# BUCKINGHAMSHIRE
# HEADLINES

★

## JEAN ARCHER

**COUNTRYSIDE BOOKS**
NEWBURY, BERKSHIRE

First Published 1992
© Jean Archer 1992
All rights reserved. No reproduction
permitted without the prior permission
of the publishers:
COUNTRYSIDE BOOKS
3 Catherine Road
Newbury, Berkshire


ISBN 1 85306 188 3
Cover Design by Mon Mohan
Produced through MRM Associates Ltd., Reading
Typeset by Paragon Typesetters, Queensferry, Clwyd
Printed in England

# Contents

# Foreword

★

The subject of this book has afforded me yet another opportunity to probe deep into the past of the county of Buckinghamshire – this time to search for stories that captured the headlines (large and small) of local and national newspapers within the last two centuries.

Research today has been made so much easier by the fact that newspapers are now on microfilm in the County Reference Library. It is now possible to sit back as if viewing television whilst page after page is presented to easy view and which can be photocopied, if desired, instead of the long, copious and weary notes of yesteryear.

Most of the stories and events contained in this book I had already noted when researching former books, and some I came upon as I progressed. The Great Chiltern Manhunt came originally from a scant story my mother related to me when I was a small child, her father in turn having told her. I was thrilled to discover it had been headline material and to have the whole story unfold.

I was astonished and somewhat shamed to realise that the Bucks Tornado of 1950 happened without my knowledge. I was living at Amersham at the time! In some cases I have striven to show how some disasters had their effect across the county i.e. the two cholera epidemics of the last century.

As usual there are many people to whom I am extremely grateful for their assistance whilst I was writing this book. Firstly, the publishers, Countryside Books themselves, who always come up with such good ideas and present an intriguing title which excites my interest immediately.

I am also grateful to those local newspapers, past and present, whose coverage of stories 'of uncommon interest' has served to focus the eyes of the nation upon Buckinghamshire. This book is dedicated to them. They include *The Chesham Examiner; Amersham and Rickmansworth Times; The Bucks Examiner; The Bucks Herald; The Buckinghamshire Advertiser; The Bucks Advertiser and Aylesbury News; The Bucks Free Press; The Wolverton Express; The Northampton Herald.*

I would especially like to acknowledge those books whose contents have been valuable to me in my research:

*History of Aylesbury* Robert Gibbs (Minet 1971)

*Olney Past and Present* O. Ratcliff and Herbert Brown (The Cowper Press 1893)

*The Aylesbury Agitator* John R. Millburn and Keith Jarrott (Bucks County Council 1988)

*Verdict on a Lost Flier* Ralph Barker (Harrup)

*No Fear nor Favour* Robert Perrin (Bucks Free Press Group 1986)

*The Hanslope Park Tragedy* French Lt. Col. The Hon. Edward Gerald (The Hove Shirley Press Ltd 1968)

My thanks also to many individuals for their help and kindness such as Mr J R Millburn; County Councillor F A Goodson and Fred Hibberd of Wendover; Nancy Sanders, formerly of Olney; John Archer; the staff of Amersham and Wendover Libraries; the County Reference Library; the Buckinghamshire Record Office; and once again my two friends, Meg Green and Dorothy Hart.

Jean Archer
Amersham, August 1992.

5

6

# The Case of the Musical Milkman

★

Most milkmen are musical. They come whistling up the garden path to the accompaniment of jingling milk bottles. But George Bailey went one step further. He claimed to have invented a new system of musical notation that was more efficient and easier to learn than the one that had been in existence from the year dot. It held no sharps or flats and could be written in one key. But just what this new system had to do with the figures of young women, he didn't say. Nevertheless, he was absolutely convinced of its revolutionary powers and remained so until the day he died – on the scaffold!

It was in the year 1920 that he came to Buckinghamshire to work for Mr Hall, a dairyman of Bourne End. He, his wife and small child lived first at Furlong Road, Bourne End, later moving to Barn Cottage near Little Marlow Church.

And it was in that August that the first advertisements began to appear in the *Bucks Free Press:* 'Young ladies, not under 16, must be over 5 ft 6 ins, well built, slim build. Applicants below height specified please state qualifications as to appearance, etc. Required for highly paid specialised work – inside and out. Applications from all classes entertained, as duties will be taught.' And applicants were required to write to a box called 'Snap'.

One would think that any girl of the present day, let alone a well brought up girl of those demure days, could not fail to look on such an advert as odd, to say the least. But still, several applicants responded from quite a wide area which took in Wycombe, Marlow, Bourne End and other places.

In particular, a Miss Marks, having become bored with her humdrum life as a grocery assistant, was one. She received instructions to attend an interview with Bailey at Bourne End, during which time he confided his ambitious plans to her. He intended to turn the cottage to which he was moving at Little Marlow into a musical academy and to teach young women with delectable figures his new system, after which they, in turn, could be teachers. He went on to say that it was remarkably easy to learn. In fact, it could be learned thoroughly within a fortnight.

After requesting her to remove her coat so that he could decide whether her figure was good enough for the job, he said she could start work on the 29th September. She was to report on that date to the cottage at Little Marlow where she was to stay for two or three nights a week, where other young ladies also selected would be staying.

Sure enough, early on the morning of 29th September, Miss Marks knocked on the door of the cottage. She was admitted and introduced to two other young ladies by the names of Miss Edwards and Miss Field, who proceeded to disappear from that moment on. Bailey then gave Miss Marks a lesson on his new system which lasted until 1 pm. Now and then she heard a child talking and caught a glimpse of a woman in an apron as she passed the door. Bailey gave Miss Marks four shillings to go out to lunch and told her not to return until 7 pm. He added that Miss Edwards and

8

*Barn Cottage, Little Marlow.*

Miss Field would be returning the following morning about 8.30 am.

Miss Marks did exactly as she was asked, seemingly having no doubts whatsoever as to Bailey's motives. She killed time in Marlow and returned to the cottage at 7 pm on the dot.

Bailey told her that two young ladies from Scotland had arrived but, being very tired, had gone to bed. After supper, Miss Marks asked to go to her room. As she climbed the cottage stairs, she heard a child crying and said to Bailey she would go and comfort it. He hurriedly and emphatically answered no, he would see to it.

Seemingly unworried and unruffled, the young lady was climbing into bed when she heard Bailey pacing up and down the stairs like a caged lion. He popped his head into the room to say that if the child cried in the night it would be necessary for him to pass through her room. She then noticed there was no lock to the door, only a latch. As she blew out the light, she surely must have felt the first pangs of apprehension. If she did not then, she must have done so later when in the moonlit bedroom she heard and saw the latch move.

Most girls by now would have been seriously alarmed, but not Miss Marks. She particularly noticed as Bailey passed through her room that he was not wearing boots.

On his way back, she feigned sleep and, through narrowed eyelids, she saw him bend over her bed and whisper 'Miss Marks, have I disturbed you?' He repeated the question louder and said the child had cried. 'Oh, no it did not' she replied, 'for I should have heard it.' He said he was going to ask her a very great favour. Girls of lesser nerve would have been out of the bedroom and half way down the stairs. Not Miss Marks. She asked him what it was. He said he wanted to sit on the chair by the door, which he did, and commenced to make idle conversation, until it turned to 'How did she like the cottage?' and then 'How would you like to be mistress of the cottage?' Oh, thought Miss Marks, he is going to propose.

But his next advance put any such thought clean out of her head. He proceeded to get into bed with her and made several attempts to 'commit an offence'. She struggled to get up but was flung back on the bed. She made it to the window and called for help. He told her it would be to no avail as there was no-one near enough to hear. She told him what he had known from the outset; that he had tricked her and no other girls were going to stay in the house. He confessed it and said quite openly he had come to her room in order to make her the mother of his children. She was shaken to the core and he stayed in her room until eight o'clock the next morning.

The truly amazing part is − the next morning she asked him if she could get the breakfast. Afterwards he brought the child to her and said the mother was unwell.

He then asked Miss Marks if she would go to the village shop to buy something for their lunch and he gave her six shillings and sixpence to do so. He informed her that both Miss Field and Miss Edwards would be at the cottage when she returned.

They arrived, in fact, mid-morning. She let them in and showed them into the sitting room. Then she decided that she had had enough. She put on her hat and coat and left by the back door to walk to Cores End where she made a complaint to the local vicar.

The Reverend gentleman quite rightly lost no time in contacting the police. Superintendent Kirby of the Wycombe County Constabulary, accompanied by Inspector West of Marlow, arrived at the cottage to find the doors locked but several windows open, through which access was made. Inside, a table was laid for tea with bread, butter and jam − there was nothing untoward in the downstairs rooms. Of Bailey and the child there was no sign, but in one of the upstairs rooms, the one next to that occupied by Miss Marks the previous night, there stood a camp bed covered with a counterpane. Under the bed was something wrapped in a sheet. It was the discoloured body of a woman − Mrs Bailey. Her husband had not been exaggerating when he had said she was unwell − she was well and truly deceased!

A post mortem was held in the cottage itself and it is interesting to note that a Dr Spilsbury was present. He

*The arrested George Bailey alights from the train at Bourne End.*

was later known as Sir Bernard Spilsbury, the famous Home Office pathologist. It was revealed that Mrs Bailey, in her twenties, was heavily pregnant with a second child, and had died of poisoning through the efficient agency of prussic acid.

A description of her husband, George Bailey, was circulated. He had in fact taken off with the child for Swindon in order to leave it with his mother. He was caught and arrested at Reading Station on his return journey and taken to Marlow where he was charged with the wilful murder of his wife. He made no reply and was conveyed to Oxford prison.

Four bottles of poison were found on him when arrested, together with a letter addressed to the Coroner which gave the impression that it may have been that Mrs Bailey had fulfilled her part of a two-way suicide pact, and that Bailey had changed his mind about his part. But the letter was mainly pre-occupied with his musical notation system. He entreated the Coroner to look after his music even though jealousy and prejudice might be encountered, as it was the system of the future. He said he had heard his wife die on the evening of 29th September – the very day that the prim Miss Marks had arrived clutching her portmanteau.

At the trial it came to light that Bailey had led a chequered life to say the least. Born at West Hampstead in 1888, it seems he had become a habitual petty criminal from an early date, in and out of prison most of the time. Thief, embezzler, conman, dealing in forgery and fraud – you name it, he had done it! He had first become a milkman in 1913 working for the Express Dairy Company, but he had embezzled their monies and absconded. He was sentenced to six months' hard labour for this offence. In 1917 he was sentenced to three years' penal servitude for forgery and larceny and his unfortunate wife, Kate, charged with passing forged cheques at his request, was also sent to prison where her first baby was born.

It transpired that Bailey had first given 'stramonia' to his wife in a cup of tea and, when she felt ill, induced her to go to bed. Whilst she lay there, he gave her prussic acid. He must have felt some pity for her sufferings, for he then administered chloroform. After she had fallen back dead, he placed beside her on the bed her three year old child, also chloroformed, and then proceeded to pass the rest of the night as related in detail by Miss Marks. Her testimony did not help him and he was sentenced to death. Whilst addressing the jury, the Judge mentioned an interesting point. He said they were the first mixed sex jury to adjudicate upon a murder trial. He added that it was certainly the first time he had ever addressed a jury which included three British women and mentioned a report in an illustrated paper which had stated that the women jurors appeared to be more interested in the proceedings than the men – a male juror had fallen asleep!

Whilst awaiting the awesome hour, Bailey did show some concern for his soon to be orphaned child, but much more for his music. Entreating everyone – 'Do not let my music die' – he died by hanging on the morning of March 2nd, 1921.

# The Great Chiltern Manhunt

★

The night of Saturday, 12th December 1891 was a moonlit, boisterous one and the wind bent the trees this way and that. It was a night that was particularly favourable to poaching operations, and the murder of two gamekeepers took place at the edge of Stocks Wood, close to Lord Brownlow's Park at Ashridge on land let to Mr Williams of Pendley Manor. It was almost directly on the Bucks/Herts border, in the Parish of Pitstone, and only 150 yards within the County of Buckinghamshire.

The bodies of William Puddephatt (keeper) and Joseph Crawley (night watchman) were not discovered until approximately 11 o'clock the next morning. They had lain in the rain and pools of blood for several hours before the head keeper and his helper stumbled across the heavy greatcoat of Crawley, just outside the wood, and the coat of Puddephatt, with a cape, lying a little further up the hill. A few more yards and they found the bodies. Both had been shockingly battered and part of a broken gun was lying near. It was plain that Crawley had been disabled by a blow, breaking his right arm before being beaten, and that Puddephatt had turned to run for assistance before he too was felled by a blow to the back of the head. Both men had carried heavy sticks with them but no guns. Tracks were seen across the fields leading to Ivinghoe, but the continuous rain had almost obliterated them. Both men came from Aldbury and the bodies were carried to a public house in that village.

This brought about a slight 'hiccup' with regard to the inquest. Detective Chief Constable Webb of Aylesbury on arrival assumed the superintendence of police enquiries, but as the bodies had been removed to Aldbury, just inside the Herts border, the duty of warning the Coroner fell to the Herts police, and it was the Coroner for that part of Hertfordshire who conducted the inquest.

It was widely known that three habitual poachers from Tring had been seen on that windy night near the canal bridge, heading for the woods where the murders were committed. Their names were Eggleton, Rayner and Smith. It was assumed that the keepers had heard a shot fired and, casting off their heavy overcoats, had given chase to the poachers and an affray had ensued.

There was no doubt in the minds of the local people who the guilty men were. In fact, during the fight in which the killing had taken place, the poacher called Smith had run for home. Early the following morning Eggleton and Rayner called at his house, to be told by his wife that he was in bed. They asked her to wake him, presumably so that he could go on the run with them, but the wise woman refused to do so and even threatened to call the police if they did not clear off. Smith stayed in bed all day Sunday and was arrested as he went to work on the Monday.

At about 8.30 am on that same Sunday morning, Eggleton and Rayner were seen in Tring, perhaps picking up food, as they then made for the thick Chiltern forests and woods.

The great Chiltern manhunt was on! It was to last eight days and nights and engage the greater part of the

County police force. So enormous was the draw on police resources during that time, only two constables were left in Aylesbury and, during the Aylesbury Petty Sessions, two men were discharged for minor offences rather than have officers spared from their duties on the hunt to give evidence.

The whole countryside was fastened in a grip of excitement and fear. Poachers were usually the heroes of the people and keepers the villains – but murder was another thing! The people locked their shutters and doors at night and kept their children close.

Later on that Sunday morning, a farmer at Wendover was talking to his shepherd in a field when they became aware of two men behaving in a furtive manner as they emerged from the woods upon the hill. Immediately they realised they had been observed, the men ran once more for the cover of the woods. The bulk of the police force rushed to Wendover and, assisted by local beaters, endeavoured to drive the men out of the woods. Several times during the next few days they came close upon the men or heard of them being a short distance off. The two must have been really adept at evasive action for the next sighting of them was at High Wycombe, where the hunt drove them into Oxfordshire. Here they actually found work threshing, but were arrested by the Oxfordshire police who promptly measured their height. But as this did not conform to the figures officially issued, they let them go!

The constable who had made the arrest felt certain they were the suspected murderers and reported the matter to his chief, who sent him back to the threshing machine with orders to re-arrest the two men. They easily spotted him coming a mile off and took to their heels. The constable gave chase, and they were rapidly outdistancing him when he espied a pony in a field.

Throwing off his tunic and helmet, he mounted it and rode bareback in hot pursuit. Just his luck the pony was already broken winded, yet still it was reported he followed the pair for twelve miles, which would seem somewhat miraculous on a pony in such a condition! The pony ultimately broke down completely, and it was said afterwards the officer found the utmost difficulty in sitting down for almost two weeks.

Due to incidents such as this, the fugitives were driven back into Buckinghamshire by way of Denner Hill and Hughenden where they met a man called Jennings, in whom, for some inexplicable reason, they confided. They told him they knew they had killed one man but did not know about the other. Needless to say, Jennings later gave evidence against them at their trial.

By the Wednesday, it had been deduced by the police that the murder weapon had definitely been a gunstock, but it had not been found and the decision was taken that as the suspected men had been seen near the canal bridge late on the night of the 12th, it would be wise to drag the canal at or near that spot.

It took some hours, but at the very time that the melancholy tolling of the bell at Aldbury Church betokened the burial of the victims, the gunstock was actually recovered from the water. It bore marks that would lead to its identification and would be an important link in the chain of evidence.

On Saturday, the 19th, it was reported that the Missendens were in a high state of excitement after a sighting of the men in that vicinity had been reported. A great force of police under Superintendent Webb descended on the area and, joined by men from both Great and Little Missenden, a wide search was soon underway. Apparently Eggleton and Rayner had been spotted coming down from Cobblers Hill onto the new railway line which was then in the course of construction in the Misbourne Valley. They had then been seen to proceed along the line towards Amersham. It was said that at the Nags Head on the Amersham Road the men had been served with bread and cheese. The next reports were that they had doubled back to Prestwood where they had received a shave and a wash, and a man said to be Rayner had been seen leaving a Prestwood farm. Police rushed to the spot and arrested a trembling 'navvy' who had been on his way to Little Kingshill, via what he thought was a short cut, to visit his girlfriend.

On Saturday night and Sunday morning police were heavily engaged in searching the countryside around Chesham and by now scores of sightings were coming in so thick and fast, and from so many different places, it was judged the hunt was getting a little out of hand due to false reports.

Police proceeded to the neighbourhood of Amersham, Beaconsfield and then on towards Slough. Superintendent Sutton, in charge of the Denham section, based on information received, became convinced that the men were somewhere within his area and he requested that forthwith the bulk of the force should search it thoroughly. Police were thick everywhere when two men went into a public house at Denham and sold a knife in order to purchase a herring, which it was reported they cooked in the house and consumed with relish.

It was here that they managed to pick up a newspaper and read for the first time the account of the murders and their own descriptions. They legged it as quickly as they could to Long Farm and hid themselves away. They emerged on Monday morning thinking the coast was clear. They were immediately arrested by Police

## EXECUTION OF THE BUCKS. POACHERS.

The condemned poachers, Rayner and Eggleton, were executed at Oxford gaol on Thursday morning. Billington, the executioner, entered Eggleton's cell at five minutes to eight, and after pinioning him proceeded to an adjoining cell, in which Rayner was confined, and quickly performed a similar operation. Both convicts wished Mr. Pullan, the chief warder, "goodbye" before leaving the cells, and thanked him and Rev. J. Knight-Newton, the chaplain, and the officials generally, for their great kindness to them. The procession was then formed, the chaplain reading the service commencing "I am the Resurrection and the Life." Rayner, who was wearing a brown billycock hat, went first, followed closely by warders, and then came Eggleton. After traversing a corridor about 15 yards long, the drop was reached. The scene was quickly over.

Both men showed great firmness, and repeated with fervency the responses to the chaplain. In about half a minute the bolt was drawn and the men disappeared from view. Not the slightest movement of the bodies was perceived. Rayner, who was slightly the taller, had a drop of 7ft., while Eggleton was given three inches less. Reporters were admitted to the execution.

*Execution notice, from* The Chesham Examiner *17th March 1892.*

Constable Payne of the Bucks Constabulary. The great Chiltern manhunt was over, and the people of the hills could rest easy once more in their beds. P.C. Payne was treated as a hero for the rest of his life.

The two poachers were taken first to Slough and then by train to Aylesbury, closely guarded by many constables. At this point feelings were still high against the men and, although the police did everything they could to keep the arrest secret until the prisoners were safely lodged in Aylesbury gaol, it seemed absolutely nothing could stop the news spreading like wildfire all along the line. At Wycombe the train was mobbed and at Princes Risborough there was a particularly hostile demonstration.

At Aylesbury Station a crowd of several hundred people gathered and although closely guarded by police, the men were hurried through the booking office and into a waiting cab, which was also surrounded by constables. Despite this, a large crowd, hooting and shouting, followed the vehicle to the police station. It was not surprising that, after eight days and nights on the run in the Chiltern Hills, coupled with their unfavourable reception, it was reported that the men looked pinched and ill.

The trial took place at the end of February 1892. All three poachers were charged with murder and tried together. Smith had run for home whilst the 'scrimmage' was taking place. Eggleton stated that he had received a blow on the head which had knocked him out for a while and that up to the time he had lost consciousness, the two keepers were alive. This did nothing to help the predicament of his friend, Rayner, who stated that he too had received a blow on the head which had rendered him unconscious. He went on to say that when he 'came to' Eggleton told him that he had broken his gun and that he had 'done for one'. He said that Eggleton then went back and killed the other in case they were later recognised. Furthermore, he added the horrific fact that Eggleton had told him 'I know he's dead 'cos I put my finger in his brains'. At this stage the stories of the two linked when they said they had then made off and thrown the gunstock into the canal.

The trial caused a great deal of controversy through-out the country for the Game Laws were most unpopular at the time, as were the landowners who bred the game. It was thought that as most magistrates were local landowners, poachers were not given a fair, unbiased trial.

Nevertheless, Smith was found guilty of man-slaughter and sentenced to twenty years. Eggleton and Rayner were found guilty of murder and sentenced to death. Both protested their innocence in court stating that they fought only in self-defence as the keepers had ferociously attacked them first with heavy cudgels, and that they had certainly not intended to kill anyone.

Both waved to sobbing females in the gallery as they turned to be led to the cells. Rayner kissed his hand and called that he 'went innocent'. They were afterwards taken to Oxford gaol where the sentence was due to be carried out on 17th March.

Many letters of protest at the sentence appeared in both the national and local press and a memorial (a statement and petition) was sent to the Home Office asking for commutation. Questions were even asked in the House of Commons. But it all went for nothing and on 17th March 1892 the sentence of death by hanging was carried out on the two unfortunate men. The press were allowed in to witness. It was reported that both Eggleton and Rayner had shown great firmness and repeated with fervency the responses to the chaplain. They then thanked all for being kind to them during their time in prison and stood bravely erect whilst the bolt was drawn.

It is to be wondered what were their last thoughts. Did they think of those days and nights deep in the Chiltern woods when they were hunted like animals at every turn, running across fields and meadows, fording streams, sleeping rough in haystacks and under hedges? Did they think about the merry dance they had led everyone, including the entire Buckinghamshire police force for over a week? Certainly there has never been quite such a hunt before or since.

# The Bucks Tornado

★

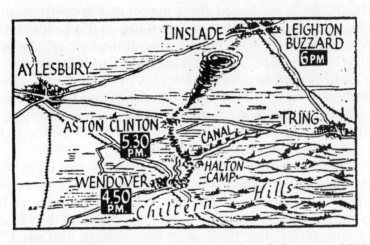

A tornado in Buckinghamshire, up until the year 1950, would have made very unfamiliar reading. Most people knew it was a remarkable and frightening phenomenon, a rapidly rotating vortex of air that sucked up everything in its path, but such happenings were usually associated with far distant climes and did not disturb them too much.

Yet – on opening their *Bucks Advertiser* on 26th May 1950, they were astonished to read the following headlines:

'SCAR TWENTY YARDS WIDE ACROSS THE FACE OF BUCKINGHAMSHIRE' 'A Tornado ripped its stormy path on Sunday afternoon and now there is a trail of damage through Wendover, Halton Camp, Aston Clinton and out through Linslade to Bedfordshire.'

It had all started at teatime in peaceful Wendover on Sunday, 21st May 1950. It had been a warm, spring day; teacups were rattling and rock cakes passed around when, over the Chilterns, clouds began to gather and darken. Just a spring storm, thought the people, as rain began to patter in the street. But those clouds began to churn and move in all directions in a way that had not been seen before.

Suddenly, out of this amazing sky, came a gigantic, monstrous spiral, swirling upwards like a giant ice-cream cone, lifting and tossing everything in its path.

Small Dean was the first to feel its force when it lifted the roof off a barn and carried it 30 feet. It seemed to hover for a moment, looking down on Wendover, then terrifying, tempestuous and, making a noise like an express train going through a station, it bore down on the tranquil town.

As an opener, it took the roof off the Baptist Chapel, tossed huge elms and chestnut trees twelve feet in the air and, in a swirl of dust and debris, began its north-easterly rampage.

The next roof to fly into the air was that of a builder's store where seven tons of concrete began to set. A massive elm crashed through the churchyard wall, narrowly missing the well-known clock tower by only a few feet, and blocking the main London-Aylesbury Road.

Up went the roof on the butchers', and tiles in their hundreds came off the half-timbered houses in Aylesbury Street. Debris was everywhere. The Landlady of The George Inn rushed to close a back bedroom window, when down crashed the roof into the bedroom, covering her with plaster and the contents of a burst hot water pipe. A single wardrobe was left to prop up the remainder of the ceiling.

One housewife was about to enter her scullery when it blew clean away in front of her eyes. Furniture jumped up and down as if possessed. A gate twelve feet high was carried twenty yards up the High Street and a line of washing disappeared over the Vale of Aylesbury never to be seen again.

The noise from the tornado was horrifying. As one woman said afterwards: 'When I heard it, I clutched my children close. I thought it was the end'.

It tore down Wharf Road, just missing the Gasometer and set off towards Halton RAF Camp. People watched as it rampaged across Wharf Meadows wafting sheds, boxes, timber and branches high up in the air. As if in fun, it lifted two horses up from one meadow and put them down in another!

At Halton Camp, two planes were lifted from the airfield as if they were toys, and others were torn from their moorings. All power had to be cut as the roof of the power house was torn off and a telegraph pole ploughed through the bakery roof. Three trees were felled by one sheet of corrugated iron. The Air Force Cadets watched as the tornado wound its way over Aston Hill in a cloud of smoke.

Now it was the village of Aston Clinton's turn where one old gentleman related, 'I was just having my tea when I saw chestnut branches and pieces of slate flying about outside the window. What's that, I thought, then a big tree fell on the house and knocked the chimney off. Then another tree, quite 150 feet tall, split in half – both pieces just missed my garage'.

The tornado had a high old time demolishing fences along the main road and pushing a 60 ft pine into the girls' school. Showing no sexual preference, it tossed pieces of coping weighing a hundredweight into the boys' school. The whole building looked as if it had

25

been turned askew. There were no complaints from the children who did not have to attend school for days afterwards. Several house tops were ripped open and television aerials were twisted into grotesque shapes. Goalposts in the recreation ground were whisked clean out of their sockets by the great, sucking wind.

The village policeman could not believe his eyes when he looked up to see a horsebox with a pony inside travelling along at a great rate all of 20 feet high in the air. The pony looked down at him in a puzzled manner before the box was brought to earth. Happily the pony was unhurt.

The farmer at Gingers Farm, which suffered extensive damage, said: 'I had just finished milking when it struck, and it frightened the life out of me. I hung on to the door post to stop myself going up in the air. I thought the cows were going to stampede but luckily they were all chained up – and, thank God, so was the bull!'

A high voltage pole near the Baptist Church was snapped in half and fuses blown.

It is interesting to note that the school clock stopped at 5.16 pm, just eleven minutes after the tornado first attacked Wendover.

On rushed the snarling, roaring monster to Puttenham where a dutch barn was completely wrecked and a cowshed flattened. The most amazing sight was that of a large chickenhouse containing all of 700 chickens which was whirled high into the air in fluttering, squawking confusion. It sped along at an alarming speed for a mile and a half when it was flung on to another farm. All that was found afterwards were the smallest pieces of the chickenhouse, and it was reported that at least five hundred chickens were either killed or missing. Sheets of corrugated iron were found

*A twisted mass of timber, steel, wood and brick on the farm belonging to the Chief Constable, Col. Warren at Puttenham.* (Bucks Advertiser)

high in tree tops hundreds of yards away.

At Linslade, 300 houses and several shops were damaged as was the parish church tower. But it was here that the tornado really spent out its fury, for it disappeared over the Bedfordshire border and petered out.

In all, it had ploughed twelve miles through the Buckinghamshire countryside and had taken about an hour to travel from Wendover to Leighton Buzzard. It had zig-zagged, but never went more than 200 yards either side of its main track. Some people within 100 yards of it were completely unaware of its passing, yet the devastation it left in its wake was comparable to the aftermath of the 'blitz'.

Immediately following came storms with hailstones 'as big as tulip heads', sharp and jagged, one weighing one and a half ounces. It took just five to fill a saucer. The Meteorological Office afterwards officially announced these hailstones as being six and a half inches round and made up of an irregular mass of ice with several centres.

An SOS was sent out for tarpaulins to cover the countless buildings minus roofs. Over 100 firemen together with helpers worked frantically rigging up temporary protection over drenched bedrooms. Nearly 800 salvage sheets and tarpaulins, some borrowed from the Ministry of Works, some from British Rail and some from local farms, were used for over 500 damaged properties.

And the onslaught was not over. Down came the rain; heavy, pelting, continuous rain, causing flood waters to swell and swirl in the town of Aylesbury and roads and villages in the locality. Traffic was thrown into chaos as the Aylesbury – Leighton Buzzard road became impassable and storm water from the Chilterns flooded the Halton-Tring road. Buses and trains were cancelled, and people fought to keep the waters from their doors. One man was trapped in a shed in a field all night as farmyards were flooded, ditches overflowed and basement supplies of coal and coke were lost.

Flood was not the only problem. At Bierton there was an extraordinary clap of thunder followed by 'a great ball of fire' which rollocked around a field then disappeared up an alley. Lightning blew high tension fuses in the storm area, adding to Aston Clinton's troubles and cutting off current to places as far afield as Bierton, Hulcott, Weedon Hill, Long Marston, Wilstone, Broughton, Boarstall and Thame. Straw from scattered ricks had blown around high voltage wires and cut off the supply to Tring for one and a quarter hours. Two sections of low voltage line were damaged by falling trees and flying debris.

At Wendover a telegraph pole carrying a high voltage line had snapped like matchwood and many service lines were broken. Technicians worked until well into the night. Firemen and helpers continued toiling non-stop for 36 hours with the aid of searchlights. One fireman was severely injured when he fell from a roof at Wendover, and three other casualties among them were reported, but they were treated on the spot and carried on. Fire appliances were called from the neighbouring counties of Beds, Berks, Middlesex and London.

In the evening of that terrible Sunday, people in Wendover stood about in groups talking over their experiences until the church bell called them to service. The George Inn, with hardly any back to the building, opened as usual.

It seemed remarkable that the tornado itself had caused no human casualties, but it had generated over £30,000 worth of damage, which was considerable in those days.

On the following Monday, Parish and District Councils and the County Council feverishly called meetings to listen to reports and delve into what went wrong with storm and flood defences, although how such a phenomenon as a tornado could have been envisaged is difficult to comprehend. Nevertheless, the County Surveyor was called upon to deliver a report as soon as possible, and it was decided that a Relief Fund should be put into action by the Mayor of Aylesbury.

Various correspondents wrote into the local newspapers stating that this tornado of 21st May 1950 was certainly not the first of such freaks of weather to have occurred in the Chilterns, though it was definitely the worst. A cyclone had caused excitement near Aylesbury in 1883 and in 1938 a tornado had raced along a path from Boxmoor in Hertfordshire to Whipsnade, Bedfordshire.

The Meteorological Office said: 'Tornadoes are rare in Britain, although similar effects are not uncommonly seen in the base of thunderstorm cloud masses and at cold fronts where exceptional turbulence is present'. The statement went on to give the official description of the occurrence as having been caused by an 'incipient tornado'. Incipient or not, the sheer ferocity of this terrifying whirlwind will never be forgotten by those who stood in its path.

# The Mysterious Fire At Coleshill

★

The evening of the 5th January 1914 was crisp and cold with patches of ice lying here and there on the roads and lanes, but Lizzie and Arthur Slade, a young couple in their early twenties, did not seem to mind. They swung along arm-in-arm towards their cottage home, laughing and chattering, happy in the company of each other, blissfully unaware of the terrible fate that awaited them before the night was out.

Some two years earlier they had been the first to be married in the newly licensed All Saints Church in the village of Coleshill and, despite the fact that their first and only baby had died, their youth and affection helped them over the tragedy. As witnesses were later to say, a more loving couple did not exist.

Their cottage was one of two built of brick, stone and tile situated at the edge of the common on the road leading from the Magpies Public House to the neighbouring village of Winchmore Hill. There were four rooms in each, two up two down, with wash-house accommodation in the shape of lean-to buildings. In the second cottage lived Ben Wingrove, his wife and three children.

That night Ben had followed his children early to bed around 7.30 pm, leaving his wife sewing by the meagre light of a tiny lamp. In such small dwellings it was possible to hear one another's movements and, at approximately 8 pm Flo Wingrove heard the young Slades enter their home. At 9.30 pm she heard them ascend the stairs to bed. By 11 o'clock her eyes had tired from the strain and she turned down the lamp and went to bed. All was quiet in those cottages at the edge of Coleshill Common.

Flo Wingrove drifted gently off into a pleasant sleep only to be suddenly awakened by a persistent tapping. Later she was unable to identify from whence it came. She did not think it was from the wall separating the two cottages.

It stopped, and she had dozed off again when she was instantly awake. There it was again – tap, tap, tap-tap, tap. What on earth was it? Nothing would wake the snoring Ben at her side. It was no good, she heaved herself out of bed and went to the window – she looked along at the cottage next door. What she saw made her scream for Ben – the Slades' cottage was in flames. She and Ben raced downstairs and outside. Both distinctly heard the voice of Lizzie Slade shout 'Come and help us'.

'Jump, Lizzie, jump,' called Flo Wingrove, 'we'll catch you.' But the front bedroom window remained firmly closed and no person appeared there. It was later established that the windows were of a sash type which slid from the side and were easy to open. Furthermore they were only seven to eight feet from the ground.

Ben kicked in the front door to be met by a wall of flame. He rushed round to the back door and repeated the process with the same result. From the back bedroom window smoke was billowing but the lean-to wash-house roof was a mere couple of feet below it and sloped down to only three or four feet from the ground. It would be simplicity itself for anyone to escape that way.

Lizzie Slade's voice came again above the crackling of the flames: 'Ben, Ben, pray get me out.'

'Go to the back' shouted Ben. He shouted until he was hoarse but at no time was the window opened nor was there anyone to be seen, and the voice of Lizzie Slade was never heard again.

The fire now had a hold on his own cottage and his children had been brought to safety. Villagers arrived on the scene and one proud possessor of a motor car sped off to Amersham, some two miles away, to call the Fire Brigade. Some were throwing water on to the Slades' cottage and others were attempting to save some of Ben's furniture, but only one or two pieces on the ground floor could be retrieved.

Young Bob Paine grabbed a ladder and reared it up to the front bedroom window from whence had been heard Lizzie's voice, but the flames were too great. He was more successful against the back bedroom window and he climbed the ladder and broke the window, but the smoke drove him back. Undaunted, he tried again and managed to see inside the room. The inner bedroom door was well and truly alight and illuminated the whole room, which was so small he said he could have stretched out his arm and touched the opposite wall. He was sure there was no-one in the room.

Choking and spluttering he made to descend, when a black cat darted without warning out of the window, past his head and up the roof behind the chimney where it shrieked and wailed with terror. The young hero climbed up onto the roof and carried the frightened animal in his arms down to safety.

It was now only 11.15 pm, and both cottages were alight from top to bottom. The heat was unbearable and no-one could get close enough to throw even the ineffectual bucket of water. There was a rending, crashing sound as first the ceiling, then the bedroom floor collapsed in a mass of burning debris. Onlookers could clearly see the bedstead go with it, some said carrying two bodies. Bob Paine definitely saw one body with its arms above its head.

In 1914 the Amersham Fire Brigade possessed only a horse-drawn fire engine and a manual pump. On the night of 5th January, they had answered the call promptly enough but the steep hill to Coleshill hampered their progress. When they arrived at the scene the cottages were a smouldering mass and water was in short supply. All they could do was to play a hose on the ruins.

Only the week before a house at Holmer Green was 'burned out' and just the outer walls were left standing. The *Bucks Examiner* reported once again that the Amersham Fire Brigade mustered promptly but could not quickly get to the scene owing 'to the delay in obtaining horses'.

By the next morning, 6th January, both in the national and local press it was reported only one wall of the cottages at Coleshill remained standing but the photograph taken at that time rather conflicts with this as there appears to be two walls standing. Nevertheless, the cottages were gutted and, after removing some six feet of debris, police came across the charred remains of Lizzie and Arthur Slade. The young couple were lying face down in opposite directions, the arms and legs were missing and they were beyond identification. The remains of the bed were close by. Prayers were said on the spot by the local vicar before the bodies were carried to The Red Lion pending the inquest. The parents of both identified various items found among the ruins, such as a watch, a ring, a woman's belt, etc.

THE MYSTERIOUS FIRE AT COLESHILL

*The cottages after the fire.*

The inquest opened at the Red Lion on the following Thursday, 9th January, under the District Coroner. The jury was made up of Coleshill names which exist in the village to this day, and the story of that disastrous night faithfully recounted by many a witness, not the least being Ben and Flo Wingrove.

It was repeatedly stated and all wondered why an easy escape had not been made by the young couple, for example from the front bedroom window which slid along to give ample aperture to jump the seven or eight feet to the ground. Or even more so from the back where the lean-to wash-house sloped to a mere three or four feet from the ground.

Also, only the voice of Lizzie Slade had been heard crying for help – not that of her husband. Why not? Was he already dead?

35

This may have been borne out by the fact that at no time did Lizzie call for Arthur, her husband, to help her. She very pointedly called to Ben, her next-door neighbour – 'Ben, pray get me out'. And what had been the source of the tapping?

The Coroner closely questioned all witnesses and stated that a number of questions would always remain unanswered; for instance, not only the origin of the fire but how the cottages came to burn so swiftly as to be a raging inferno in ten minutes. This he found truly amazing and recalled that the last fire of such nature took place at The Black Swan, High Wycombe in March 1905. On that occasion a woman and two children lost their lives.

The jury returned a verdict to the effect that Lizzie and Arthur Slade had met their deaths by suffocation and that there was no evidence to show how the cottage caught fire.

Over the last eight decades many theories as to the origin of the fire have been softly voiced. In fact, if you ask the older villagers to this day, one will say this and one will say that. Some say the tiny lamp was the cause, but the Coroner himself said he hardly thought this would create such a swift fire. Some say hot coals were carried upstairs and some say Lizzie Slade was smoking, but taking all in all it just does not seem feasible. And then one individual voiced an unusual theory – that of spontaneous human combustion, which is a well known, but unproven, phenomenon where a person suddenly bursts into flames for no apparent reason. This would to some extent explain the silence of Arthur Slade, but then again it is difficult to prove that the poor unfortunate person caused a fire of the kind experienced at the Slades' cottage on that January night.

Be that as it may, as the Coroner said all those years ago, 'What happened on that night will never be known'. And certainly the gaunt, tall gravestone covered in lichen and mould that stands at the entrance to the cemetery in Old Amersham will never tell.

# Up, Up And Away!

★

It was in the year 1891 that the High Wycombe Horticultural Society decided to hold their Annual Show on August Bank Holiday Monday. And it was also in that year that they agreed to add the attraction of amusements, which they considered would draw the crowds like never before. In previous years they had run athletic sports and Fire Brigade contests, but this year they proposed to run a tennis tournament to be played on the lawn in front of the Abbey, a team from Amersham contesting singles and doubles with the Wycombe players. Also they engaged a wire-walking expert by the name of 'Moxetia, King of the lofty tight telephone wire'.

But the item that had all the area agog with excited anticipation was a proposed balloon ascent by Professor Higgins and his lovely assistant, Miss De Voy, the well-known parachutist. It was widely advertised that these two would rise in the balloon to an astonishing height, whereupon they would launch themselves into mid-air and descend by parachute.

The Professor was well qualified, or so he said. He claimed to have made 44 ascents and to hold a gold medal presented to him by the Balloon Society of Great Britain. He recalled having descended from tremendous heights, in particular some 12,000 feet at Wolverhampton. Indeed, on one occasion at Croydon, his parachute was cut away and his balloon carried him to the astonishing height of 26,000 feet (5 miles). He ultimately came down to earth without injury at Penshurst in Kent.

Miss De Voy was also publicised as having made approximately two dozen trips through the air and on one occasion had nearly lost her life when, due to an error of judgement, she came to rest in the lake at the 'Welsh Harp', Hendon.

The use of the beautiful Wycombe Abbey Park for their Annual Show had been granted to the Horticultural Society for many years past, and this particular August Monday dawned in perfect weather. On rising ground above the avenue of limes, the usual collection of tents of various sizes presented to the eye of a visitor the semblance of an encampment on a large scale. There was the tall, spacious marquee for flowers, smaller tents for produce and refreshments, which, together with the brightly coloured stalls, presented a colourful picture.

After lunch, some 8,000 people packed the park to enjoy the programme of amusements. The tennis tournament was successful, although, after some spirited play, the Amersham team trounced the Wycombe players.

Excitement grew as the time scheduled for the wire-walking arrived. Two performances by 'Moxetia' had been advertised but only one took place, and that was a dismal failure. The great man just balanced on the wire without moving, walking or turning the usual somersaults or tricks. True he smiled winningly all the while at his audience, but it was just not enough, and the Committee of the Society were singularly disappointed.

However, thoughts were swiftly transferred to the main attraction of the day – Professor Higgins, Miss De Voy and their balloon ascent, not to mention the parachute jump.

Take off, or float off, was scheduled for 6 pm and crowds poured into the ground ready for this sensational event. In those pre-aeroplane days, the air was uncharted territory and people viewed the balloon as something almost magical as they watched it begin to inflate with gas supplied by a pipe from the main in St Mary Street. The filling proceeded very slowly indeed and, after a period of time, it became evident that something was amiss, and that unless other measures were taken, the balloon would not be ready for the six o'clock take off.

Professor Higgins averred that a partial stoppage in the main had reduced the pressure of gas which had brought about the slow inflation. In order to remedy this, the balloon was moved closer to the Gas Works where the operation of inflation recommenced. Once the balloon was full, it was intended to somehow bring it back to the park, where even more people had congregated in great numbers and, as the time reached six o'clock, and then passed, the crowd began to mutter and mumble at the delay.

Meanwhile, back at the Gas Works, the balloon was slowly expanding, though still far from full, and it was decided to send it up from the spot. The time was now approaching eight o'clock and crowds were flocking from the park to Loakes Meadow, a spot close to the proposed point of departure, drawn by the strains of the band, whose members were near the point of exhaustion.

It was obvious there was not enough lifting power in the balloon to accommodate two persons and Miss De Voy agreed to go up alone. Throwing off her cloak with a flourish, she stood revealed in braided scarlet military costume with a sash and, as she took her place on the trapeze-like attachment suspended below the balloon, a kind of weary cheer went up.

The word was given to 'Let Go', but instead of shooting upwards with a rush, the balloon remained within a yard or two of the ground and, kept down by Miss De Voy's weight, moved across the field causing something of a hazard to the crowds who now scattered in all directions. Miss De Voy flung herself off in a rather undignified manner and the balloon rose pathetically upwards just a little, but after passing over the western end of town, it fell in paroxysms of contortions and varied weird noises of extreme relief into another field.

The disappointment of the spectators was keen, to say the least, and it was said afterwards that it was only due to great restraint that mere verbal expressions of disapproval were heard and no real violence offered.

The firework display put on by Messrs Brock and Company at the end of the evening made up for quite a bit, particularly the spectacular fire fountains and waterfall, and the band summoned their flagging strength to wind up the event with a rendering of the National Anthem.

The *Bucks Free Press* printed a graphic report of the Show, and in the same paper there appeared a letter from an enraged Gas Works Manager who wished to strongly refute a report 'which had circulated the town that the failure of the balloon ascent on the Bank Holiday was due to the insufficient supply of gas'. He went on to say in no uncertain terms that the fault was 'in the balloon itself which was not gas-tight, and this was clearly proved by the fact that it received three times the quantity of gas needed to fully inflate it'.

An Inquiry by the Committee into the failure of the balloon to ascend disclosed the fact that precisely 70,000 feet of gas had been used and therefore it seemed obvious that the balloon had allowed the gas to escape. This conclusion did not please Professor Higgins who, whilst marching up and down in high dudgeon, still endeavoured to cast the blame on the Gas Company and insisted his balloon was quite sound. The fact that he could see the balance of his fee disappearing may have influenced his excitement.

Harsh words were hurled back and forth before it was eventually agreed that an independent expert should inspect the balloon in order to give an unbiased opinion as to which party was definitely at fault. Mr Lefevre, the President of the Balloon Society, was called in at a fee of two guineas on behalf of the Horticultural Association. This gentleman turned out to be well equipped with diplomacy and tact for immediately upon his arrival he stated with fervour that he had never seen a better arranged Gas Works for the size of the town. He then ventured inside the balloon and blew on the texture while another on the outside held his hand opposite, and as he blew, the one on the outside felt a current of air. It was as simple as that. The Gas Works was cleared of all blame and Mr Lefevre stated that he thought it was more Higgins' misfortune than fault as whatever knowledge he had of ballooning, he did not seem to be aware of the effects that the heat of a summer day could have on the fabric of a balloon. Apparently he should have soaked it with water.

The proposal was put to Higgins that he and his glamorous assistant should make the double ascent the following week and that he should be paid £30 on the accomplishment of the feat. At first he demurred in a sulky manner but in the end he signed an agreement.

Once more the event was advertised, the public were to be allowed free into Loakes Park in time for the ascent at 5.30 pm.

In the meantime reports of the results of at least two other unsuccessful balloon attempts appeared in national and local papers. In the first instance, parachutist Professor Baldwin had a very narrow escape from maltreatment at Paignton. Before an assembled crowd, his balloon instead of rising gracefully into the blue, had dragged along the ground and he had released his hold, letting it ascend by itself. It struggled up to a hundred yards when it turned over and fell, emitting similar noises to those experienced at High Wycombe. Like Professor Higgins, he blamed the gas, but the crowd threatened to lynch him. He escaped in great panic over a wall.

Similarly at Nottingham, before a gathered crowd of 5,000 spectators, Professor Russett's balloon failed to rise to the occasion. Having kept the crowd waiting two hours, it was announced that the failure was due to the balloon having been filled with 'impure gas'. The crowd went berserk, tore up the balloon and mobbed the Professor. Ultimately he had to be locked in the pavilion all night for his own safety.

Small wonder then that by the Friday, Professor Higgins, Miss De Voy and their balloon, had left the town of High Wycombe, no doubt as a result of having read the before-mentioned reports. On Saturday a telegram was received from him saying that unless the whole of the money was paid to him before the event, plus an extra £5 for expenses, he would not return.

The Committee decided to forget him and turned to Lieutenant Lempriere, a well-known aeronaut, to help them out of their difficulty. He undertook to perform the feat, using his own balloon and a lady parachutist by the name of Miss Cissie Kent, nineteen years old, from a theatrical family and as pretty as a picture. She also had a modest, attractive personality to match. She certainly had the *Bucks Free Press* reporter under her spell when he called at the Falcon where she was staying with Lieutenant Lempriere, and her manager. When interviewed, she had just finished luncheon and she was asked whether the prospect of her bold feat had not interfered with her appetite. She gave a tinkling laugh, which the reporter found entrancing, and told him that she had thoroughly enjoyed soup, lamb cutlets and plum pudding, washed down with a glass of claret.

The reporter wrote that it was obvious she was perfectly easy and unconcerned, and seemed to look forward to her aerial journey with positive pleasure. She had already made nine of these and her manager went so far as to say that the only fault was she was too fond of soaring aloft. So much so that when she was among the clouds, she found it so enjoyable that she was reluctant to descend. She now had the cub reporter completely 'by the ears'. He recorded that there was an entire lack of boastfulness and that she modestly disclaimed 'the possession of unusual courage'. He went on 'In fact the young lady is slim and graceful, and the refinement of her demeanour is in strong contrast to the idea some people would form of one accustomed to perform feats of daring hardihood'.

Miss Kent described her sensations whilst on one of her voyages as follows: 'Everything so far up', she said, 'is so still and quiet. The balloon revolves slowly in ascending, and I can hear the hum of human voices dying gradually away as I go up. The atmosphere is cold but exhilarating. Some sounds penetrate to great altitudes, especially the noise of railway trains. When I go up I have hold of the parachute with my left hand, and with my right I grasp the rope attached to the trapeze bar. When I leap all I do is to leave go of the bar and seize the parachute handle. At first there is a terrific rush through the air, and then a tug as the parachute expands'. She said the drop was usually quite smooth, though there were oscillations caused by successive currents of air.

The ascent was fixed for 5.30 pm – the place was the Barracks Ground in convenient proximity to the Gas Works. Absolutely no difficulty was experienced in filling the balloon this time – it took just over an hour. The Gas Works Manager watched with profound satisfaction for this proved without any doubt that the previous failure was in no way due to any fault on the part of his company.

A tremendous crowd of people had gathered in the adjacent meadows and the ground was thickly surrounded. On the hills on either side of the valley groups of spectators were visible everywhere. People were standing on the rooftops of the houses in the town, on the top of Wycombe Abbey and even on the church tower. Away on the horizon to the north, groups of people could be seen standing atop hay ricks and barns. Those who stood in close proximity included such notables as the Mayor of High Wycombe, and a rather nervous Secretary and members of the Committee of the Horticultural Society. They had good reason to feel apprehensive, for if things did not go well this time, the crowd could turn violent.

Members of the Wycombe Fire Brigade proudly held the balloon in position, and this took some doing as, in contrast to the last time, the balloon was raring to go. Cheers went up as Cissie Kent entered the ground. She looked charming clad in a knickerbocker suit of blue velvet with the most winning little cap of the same material on her head, and stockings of light pink. She

A representative of the *Free Press* had an interview with Miss Kent on the afternoon of Wednesday, and obtained some particulars of her career which will be read with interest. Calling at the Falcon Hotel, he was shown into the dining room, where Miss Kent, with Mr. Lempriere and her manager, Mr. A. Payne, had just finished luncheon. A question as to whether the prospect of her bold feat had not interfered with her appetite elicited a laughing negative, and as a proof the menu was referred to, showing that Miss Kent had partaken of soup, lamb cutlets, and plum pudding, washed down by a glass of claret. The

barometer. She was 7½ minutes in ascending, and 6½ minutes in her fall. Mr. Payne concluded by calling for three cheers for the plucky little lady, which were hastily given. The aeronauts then entered the "Lion," where they remained during the evening. For some time a crowd remained in front of the hotel, cheering for the parachutist.

Miss Kent appeared delighted with the success of her performance, and expressed to those who congratulated her afterwards her appreciation of the welcome given her on all hands. "I must show you," she said to our reporter, "my watch and medal," and she thereupon produced for inspection a handsome gold chronograph, with the monogram "C. K.," and an inscription :—"Subscribed for by the public, and presented to Miss Cissie Kent as a momento of her two successful parachute descents at Sheffield, June 4th and 7th, 1890." On the latter occasion, Miss Kent ascended to the extraordinary height of 11,000 feet. The medal was presented to her by a gentleman at Barnsley. Miss Kent promised a visit to Wycombe in the winter, if possible, with a concert party, and if her intention is carried out, she will doubtless meet with a cordial welcome.

Intelligence was received on Thursday that the balloon had been picked up at Wimbledon, in Surrey.

PHOTOGRAPHS OF THE BALLOON ASCENT.—We have inspected some excellent photographs taken by Mr. Starling of the scene on the occasion of Miss Kent's balloon ascent, as well as portraits of the parachutist in ordinary costume. Mr. Findlow has also taken some cabinet portraits of Miss Kent, and succeeded in obtaining a view of the parachute descending, though owing to the great distance the object is very minute.

*An intrepid reporter from* The South Bucks Free Press *gets a scoop by interviewing Miss Cissie Kent before her ascent. She obviously made a sizable impression on most of the crowd that day as well.*

was completely calm and confident and chatted pleasantly with the onlookers. More cheers went up as she took her seat below the balloon, firmly grasping the pendant of the parachute. There was a moment of breathless suspense and the command 'Let Go' was given by Lieutenant Lempriere, but instead of shooting up into the air, the balloon, hovering within a foot or two of the ground, was carried towards the fence on the other side of the field.

This was a very nasty moment for the Secretary and members of the Horticultural Society, not to mention the Mayor who was seen to pale visibly. Lieutenant Lempriere and the firemen brought the balloon back to its moorings, and a bag of shot and woodwork was detached with the object of lightening the load. Another attempt followed, but still the balloon was obstinate and refused to take off correctly on its journey.

The possibility of another failure loomed ominously, and the Secretary of the Society had to be supported by his colleagues, whilst the Mayor looked around for a means of escape.

But they need not have worried. The gallant Lieutenant Lempriere was equal to the emergency and called for more gas. This solved the problem, and this time when the firemen let go, the balloon, with Cissie Kent suspended underneath, rose gracefully to the loud cheers of the crowd and the intense relief of the Committee of the Horticultural Society.

A westerly breeze carried the balloon and Cissie along the Wycombe valley where it rose to a great height. The crowd craned their necks to follow its route and soon the white mushroom of the parachute billowed out as Cissie cast herself into mid-air. It fell slowly 'with its fair burden' and could be seen coming down gently towards the ground. Cissie Kent descended safely into a barley field near The Rifle Butt, alighting without the slightest difficulty. She was drawn from the spot in great style in an open carriage into the town where the streets were lined with people anxious to see and afford her a tumultuous reception. The conveyance came to a halt at The Red Lion where her Manager insisted on making a speech on her behalf, in which he stated that they had been severely handicapped by the failure of a previous attempt, and, had Miss Kent been unsuccessful, things could have been most unpleasant for all concerned. The Committee, now fortified by appropriate refreshment, nodded fervent agreement. But, he went on, Miss Kent had been successful (cheers) and had enjoyed a pleasant voyage (laughter). Three more hearty cheers for heroine Cissie were wholeheartedly and lustily given, whereupon the party entered The Red Lion and stayed there for the rest of the evening.

How wonderful it was for the Society to view the headlines of the *Bucks Free Press* the following week: 'SUCCESSFUL BALLOON ASCENT – A Drop of 6,000 feet accomplished'.

There was no doubt that the people of the town and area had taken Cissie Kent to their hearts, and before she left, she promised to return the following year, perhaps with a concert party and, said the reporter, 'she will meet with the most cordial welcome'.

The balloon was eventually picked up at Wimbledon in Surrey.

# King Cholera

★

During the year 1818 news of a terrible, fearful disease reached England for the first time. It had started in India where it was ravaging the population, including the British troops stationed there. Symptoms began with diarrhoea and vomiting followed by the most agonising pains in the abdomen and limbs. Within three to four hours fever raged, and death usually took place within a day, sometimes within a few hours. The disease was called Asiatic Cholera!

By 1830 it was rampant in Russia, and spread so rapidly that soon all the Baltic ports and most of the capitals of Europe had been affected. The British Ambassador in Russia had written home revealing in full the terrors of this new disease which he described as a sort of 'plague'.

No-one seemed to know much about it; how it started or how it was carried, but it did seem to hit the poorer sections of a city or town. This was not to say it was not lethal in the countryside as well and it was thought that filth and poor sanitation was a source of encouragement to its spread.

The people of this country watched it creep towards them from the European mainland and awaited its arrival with trepidation. They looked around at their own environment which was without proper water supplies or sewerage system, let alone refuse collection. When the streets and drains stank worse than usual, it was considered a sign of bad weather.

It is amazing to consider that 53 old cesspits were discovered under Windsor Castle and Queen Victoria's apartments at Buckingham Palace were ventilated through a sewer.

At Aylesbury, the people were thankful for the numerous pigs that roamed the streets. These animals were not only the scavengers, but also the only municipal cleansers. They ate their way through a good proportion of the refuse that was thrown 'willy nilly' from the buildings. In fact, some of the inhabitants purchased pigs solely for the purpose of turning them out on the public thoroughfares to obtain their living. Not a bad method of pig farming!

In all, cholera took 13 years to travel from India to Great Britain. In October 1831, the first official case of the disease was diagnosed in Sunderland and by November, five people had died. By January 1832 there were 3,639 cases in the north with deaths at 874.

The *Aylesbury News* reported that 'The cholera engages the serious attention of the House of Commons' and that one, Joseph Jumer, 'complained of the cant and hypocrisy of some members in ascribing the disease to Divine Providence'.

It reached London in February and tore through the 'Rookeries' – those overcrowded slum courts, heaving with humanity and filth. A mere forty miles away, the *Bucks Herald* reported that there was a 'great fright here at Aylesbury at the spread of the cholera'. It was also reported that the authorities at Hoddesdon in Hertfordshire had employed two parish beadles to keep out the contagion. The beadles were stationed at the town's ends and made all the 'grubby' looking folks go around instead of through the town. The newspaper went on 'this is like spreading a net over the houses to keep off the smallpox, or chopping up a wheelbarrow that had been bitten by a mad dog'.

By 22nd June 1832, cholera had appeared in Aylesbury with fifteen cases and five deaths. That very day, a Board of Health was hurriedly set up which was considered by some to be locking the stable door after the horse had bolted. The next night a cholera funeral took place. It was late, quite dark and a dismal sight. 'The coffin was preceded by a lantern and the procession walked fast. There were no mourners to follow and the person buried had been in good health that morning'.

The speed of the disease was terrifying. As the *Bucks Free Press* said 'The cholera has raged very alarmingly at Marlow, so much so that twelve to fifteen burials have taken place in a day. Among others, a poor man, who left his wife early in the morning well, was much surprised on his return home to learn that, during his absence, she had died of cholera and had been buried. Feeling disconsolate and dissatisfied, he betook himself to the grave and dug up the corpse. On lifting off the lid of the coffin, he was struck by the appearance of his wife and thought he perceived symptoms of life, which soon became realised as, after a while, the poor woman rose up, and to the great joy of her husband, accompanied him home, and wonderful to relate, that night became a mother'. The reporter went on 'The woman and her child are at this moment regarded by the inhabitants of Marlow as great curiosities'. This remarkable story also appeared in *The Observer*.

By 28th June there were 141 cases in Aylesbury, 15 of them fatal, which was a smaller proportion than many other places. Through the press, the people were informed that the best way to try to prevent the disease spreading was to indulge in temperate drinking only. Good but carefully cooked food was recommended, together with perfect cleanliness, a vegetable diet and abstinence from unripe fruit.

Despite this, came the 13th July it was reported that the total number of cases in Aylesbury was 229 with 50 deaths. Five cases in the gaol had terminated fatally with several serious ones still under treatment.

When no further cases were reported in Aylesbury during August, people began to breathe just that little easier, and indeed the disease had begun to abate. By the time this first epidemic of the dreaded cholera was over in this country it had carried off some 30,000 people. Clearly the inhabitants of Aylesbury had been caught more or less on the hop and yet, despite this, when it was reported to the House of Commons 17 years later in 1848 that another epidemic of cholera was moving across Europe along the same track towards this country as had the one in 1831, the ratepayers were still reluctant to review the bad sanitary and water conditions, not to mention the piles of refuse still festering in the streets. The leaders of the town were first berated and then implored to do something, but they felt they should not be called upon to pay extra towards the habitations of the poor. It was repeatedly pointed out to them that, if the disease was allowed to thrive in the hovels of the poor on the outskirts of the town, it brought the danger closer to themselves.

The *Bucks Herald* really went for those obstinate ratepayers. The Editor asked 'Is it to be borne that a town so situated for drainage as Aylesbury should be besieged with mephitic vapours, its outskirts poisoned by putrid open ditches and its most central portion tainted by the laystalls of the inns and by the obstruction of the narrow channels facetiously called its drains?'

Beside himself with indignation, he went on to

*Disease-ridden slums of the type that allowed cholera to flourish so freely.*

inform readers that the *Herald* itself was 'personally subjected to the feculent flood before our own house which every day administers to us a pungent reminder of the ill-drained and unhealthy condition of our town', and he demanded that those men who opposed improvements should make themselves known.

In the House of Commons, Lord Morpeth said he did not wish to alarm the people but the cholera was definitely on its way to the shores of Britain and he gave figures of deaths in most of the countries of Europe. He threw in that a good preventative was peppermint, brandy and pepper, whilst Mr F.W. Payne of Aylesbury advertised in the *Bucks Herald* that 'he would supply families with Elleman's Disinfecting Fluid at the wholesale price for gratuitous distribution to the poor. A whole village may have a sufficiency of this excellent preventative of contagion for a few shillings'.

If Aylesbury had not the good sense to do so, both Amersham and Chesham formed Emergency Boards of Health and sent deputations around their respective towns to inspect every dwelling. Nevertheless, it was reported on 21st October that 'the visitation of the cholera has caused great excitement at Chesham where there has been twenty cases and eight deaths'.

On 6th December, a very large meeting was held in the County Hall at Aylesbury on the Health of the Towns Bill which had recently been passed. This gave people leave to improve the sanitary conditions of their towns, but did not compel them to. W. Ranger, one of the Commissioners under the new Act, opened an inquiry into the health of the town of Aylesbury. Hero of the hour, local Dr Robert Ceely faced powerful opposition as he stated that the sickness of the lower classes was due to the sewerage around them and the want of drainage of their habitations. He bravely said that he stood there to speak for the poor of the town and added that, however unpopular it may make him, he would do his duty. He warmed to his subject as he said that it was the poor that showed the first indications of the disease and were the earliest victims. This, he said, was hardly surprising as they lived in hovels with continually damp floors and walls. He also pointed out that with disease thriving on the outskirts of the town, it ultimately affected the better off ratepayers and that they would indeed benefit by improving conditions.

The Doctor then offered to take the Commissioner around the town on a tour of inspection and said that he was confident that he could prove that the state of the poor of the town of Aylesbury was a disgrace to civilisation.

The majority of the leaders of the town present at that meeting were not pleased with the young Doctor and were still not inclined to fork out extra rates to help the poor.

A week later Mr Ranger concluded his investigation and before returning to London stated that on his return he would take up the question of the water supply. Among the poor was a feeling of deep thankfulness that at last there appeared a glimmer of hope of something being done. At Aylesbury this was one of the first commissions under the Health of the Towns Act.

January 1849 loomed and cases of 'true Asiatic Cholera continued to exhibit themselves at Chesham, much to the alarm of the residents there and the disquiet of the people in other parts of the County, including Aylesbury'. Yet, when Mr Ranger's report on the sanitary state of Aylesbury was received, it caused considerable consternation as the sum required to be expended was estimated at £17,000. Another meeting was immediately called and County Hall was densely packed with ratepayers to offer opposition to the Act itself and things went on much as before.

It was in August that cholera appeared in the cottages of Gibraltar, near Dinton, only one or two miles from Aylesbury. In no time several cases had proved fatal. Further meetings were held in Aylesbury, one in particular to deal with what steps should be taken in the event of cholera appearing in the town. Mr Ranger now published a supplementary report. His chief worry was the supply of good water – mainly due to the fact that a man called John Snow in London, who had served as an assistant during the epidemic of 1831/32, was convinced that cholera was a waterborne disease.

Mid-August and fear became sharper as the scourge of cholera was reported as running riot at Loudwater, Marlow and Wycombe. Seventeen more had died at Gibraltar and, in an attempt to escape the contagion, the people had left their cottages and were living in tents in the surrounding fields. Dr Robert Ceely described the scene as the most heart rending he had ever seen. In all, 48 persons died there out of a population of 55.

In September, the *London Gazette* contained several orders in council relative to the Public Health Act, one of which alluded to Aylesbury. As a consequence, another large meeting was called at County Hall and the election of a Local Board was proposed. This time it sailed through and was carried unanimously. This new Board superseded the old Parish Surveyors, including the administration of lighting and watching, and with the exception of the management of the poor, became more or less the governing body of the town.

Their task was not an easy one. Almost immediately they were in trouble. The old sewers terminated in different outskirts of the town, but mostly discharged themselves into the millstream. The increase in population brought about an increase in sewage and consequently the stream became polluted and adjacent landowners complained and even threatened legal proceedings.

Reports of the cholera were more cheering in October. The disease was abating and on the decline at last.

By some miracle, there were no cases at all in Aylesbury during this second epidemic of 1848/49 but by the time it had finished, the total number of deaths from the disease in Great Britain and Wales was not less than 90,000.

Cholera was and is evil and yet from these two initial epidemics came the first awareness that environment mattered, that proper sanitation, water supplies and collection of refuse were vital to health. Its deadly presence brought about the Public Health Act which was the first step to be taken in a series of Acts that improved the living and working conditions of the people.

# Outward Bound
# To Queensland

★

William and Rebecca Climpson of Chesham, together with their three children, were the first family from Buckinghamshire to travel on a Government migrant ship to Moreton Bay, Queensland, Australia. They sailed on the good ship *Artemisia*, arriving at their destination on 13th December 1848.

To emigrate at that time took a considerable amount of courage, and more than a dash of adventurous spirit. For one thing, emigrants had to be prepared to part forever from the folk they left behind, as there was practically no hope of returning. They only had a vague idea of the country to which they were travelling and what awaited them. The voyage was arduous, filled with discomfort, and with varying climates, took about four months to complete. The spur that sent them was the fact that times were desperately hard in England, and would grow worse with an increasing population.

This continual growth made the life of the agricultural labourer in particular very hard to bear. It brought about unemployment, which meant trying to live on the parish. Even those in work, living on the lowest of wages in one room hovels with no sanitation or running water, faced near starvation for their families and themselves. The position was not helped by the infamous Game Laws, under which a man could not kill a hare, rabbit or bird seen from his cottage window to feed his children without risking prison, transportation or even his life. With no hope of any improvement, despair was the byword, and they all knew the ultimate was the brutal workhouse.

A few years after the departure of the Climpson family, a thin trickle of other Buckinghamshire folk followed their example and in 1857 several families from the county emigrated.

In the 1850s, Queensland became separated from New South Wales and was proclaimed a separate colony, with its own Parliament and Governor. By 1872, this young Government's 'New Immigration Act' came into force, under which free passages were granted to certain classes of immigrants, and a local agent was appointed at Aylesbury, which largely accounts for the fact that it was to Queensland that most Bucks emigrants sailed.

The men from Bucks provided an excellent type of colonist. They were accustomed to long and tedious hours of outdoor work and could turn their hands to tree felling and any sort of rough hand work. The women were prepared to bear and rear large families.

It was not only the Queensland agent at Aylesbury who advertised and persuaded local workers to seek pastures new. They were also encouraged by the National Agricultural Labourers Union, a branch of which was formed in Bucks in 1872. It was in this year also that young Edward Richardson, schoolmaster in the tiny village of Dinton, resigned his post and became a full-time activist for the union. Meetings had already been held at Denham and Chalfont St Peter, much to the consternation of local farmers.

A good orator, Richardson was soon walking to many villages in the county to address labourers at meetings sometimes held after dark by the light of lanterns. He walked to Wendover and Princes Risborough to name but a few. In his own words 'I walk from place to place, mostly a stranger to everyone I address. My average walking amounts to 120 miles per week'. He went on to say that he frequently walked ten miles out, lectured for two hours, and then walked the ten miles home 'alone, across country and nearly midnight'. On a moonless night, in a countryside with no lights to speak of, this must have been daunting.

Richardson advised his rustic listeners that the only alternative to their dire living conditions was to emigrate to Queensland. Mostly he held his audience rapt as he talked of a freedom hitherto unknown to them, where land was cheap, and they stood a good chance of ending up their own masters. Many were won over, but he eventually decided that the only way to really encourage these simple country folk was to travel with them so he would be able to see that they were well looked after on board ship and also on their arrival in Queensland. He could then return to Bucks and report to the remainder of their families just how they were doing in the distant land.

Advertisements appeared in the local newspapers asking for 300 farm labourers, female domestic servants and any others who felt so inclined to accompany Richardson on a voyage to Queensland in mid-March 1873. Richardson followed this up with even more meetings in the villages. At some he was heckled and shouted down, at others he was welcomed and cheered.

At the village of Long Crendon, the meeting resulted in some forty persons handing in their names as being willing to accompany him, several married men with families were among them. Waddesdon produced sixteen adults and some eighteen children, all ready to

By Authority of H. M.  Government of Queensland.

## EMIGRATION TO QUEENSLAND, AUSTRALIA.

From the great demand which now exists in the Colony for all kinds of labour, the Agent-General will grant

# FREE PASSAGES

TO

## FARM-LABOURERS & FEMALE DOMESTIC SERVANTS,

*(Without undertaking for payment of cost of passage,)*

AND

# ASSISTED PASSAGES

TO

## MECHANICS AND OTHER ELIGIBLE PERSONS.

## TO INTENDING EMIGRANTS.

An unusual opportunity now presents itself to Farm-Labourers, Female Domestic Servants, and other eligible Persons desirous of Emigrating to Queensland, under the personal superintendence of Mr. E. RICHARDSON (of Aylesbury), who has made official arrangements to accompany some 300 emigrants on or about the 17th of March next.

The advantages offered are a Free Passage, Free Kit, and Railway Fare Paid. Each emigrant being required to provide the regulation quantity of clothing only. Special advantages offered to Female Servants. The increased demand for good servants has materially improved the rates of wages, which now stand as follows: Female Domestic Servants from £30 to £52 per annum. General Labourers from £30 to £50 per annum. Ploughmen from £60 to £70 per annum; with rations, consisting of 8lbs. of flour; 12lbs. of beef; 2lbs. of sugar; ¼lb. tea— weekly.

Mr. Richardson expects to return to England about November, 1873, to report upon the prospects of New Settlers in Queensland. He will also visit those persons who left Aylesbury for Brisbane, in the ship 'Storm King.'

Gentry and friends can render valuable assistance by helping boná-fide emigrants with gifts of wearing apparel, also by assisting in filling up the necessary forms.

As the responsibility of this undertaking is necessarily great, Mr. Richardson will gladly acknowledge, on behalf of the emigrants, any pecuniary help, parcels of left-off clothing, books, or other articles needed during a long voyage.

An early and personal application (if possible) should be made to Mr. E. RICHARDSON, or Mr. S. G. PAYNE, Government Agent, Aylesbury.

L. POULTON, PRINTER, MARKET SQUARE, AYLESBURY.

61

follow his leadership. The rest came in twos and threes from other villages around the Vale of Aylesbury. At Haddenham he told the meeting they had better hurry up and make up their minds, as he only had 30 places left.

It was eventually announced that 209 families, 109 single men and 51 single females would be sailing with Richardson on a ship called the *Ramsey* on 24th March 1873. Great preparations were made by friends and relations to kit out the emigrants for the voyage. Clothes were knitted and sewn for the varying climates that would be encountered, and many a Buckingham-shire mother's heart grew heavy as the time drew near for tearful farewells.

At Waddesdon a farewell service was held in the church, a separate one being held for the Wesleyan Sunday school teacher who was emigrating with his wife and three children.

At last the long awaited morning of 24th March dawned. Richardson arrived at Long Crendon shortly after first light where he collected some two dozen emigrants. Swinging along, singing farewell songs, they marched to Thame Station accepting presents and good wishes from cottagers along the way. As the train came in, there were many last handshakes and good wishes and, as it pulled out, it was cheered until it could be seen no more.

There were even more crowds at Aylesbury Station where a further 150 emigrants were saying goodbye to relations and friends when they were joined by the contingent from Thame. A farewell speech from Richardson and a loaded train jerked off in the direction of Tring. Here, another party were picked up, which completed the whole *Ramsey* shipment en route for the London Docks and the ship that was to take them to a new land.

The *Ramsey* was a vessel of 893 tons and, although said to possess an unusual appearance from the outside, her interior was equipped to accommodate emigrant families as no other ship had been up until that time. Previously, a family had been required to share a compartment with one other at least. On the *Ramsey* it was one compartment for one family. It was afterwards thought that the *Ramsey*, during her lifetime, carried more emigrants to Queensland than any other ship. Certainly she made at least 13 round trips, only to be wrecked on a homeward journey in 1883.

On 5th April 1873, the *Bucks Advertiser* reprinted a superb report of the ship's departure from the London Docks, which had appeared in the *Daily News* of 31st March:

'The good ship *Ramsey*, as trim a vessel as ever crossed the ocean, had an unusual share of farewells last Wednesday. Her decks were covered with between three to four hundred of the agricultural population of Buckinghamshire'. The report goes on: 'The sun shone bountifully and the emigrants showed no regret. Even before the ship was clear of the basin, groups of girls struck up a melody on the quarter deck while further 'forrard' a young Unionist produced a violin and drew lively music from its strings'. These Bucks workers, who had faced near starvation diets at home, were 'open mouthed at the piles of beef, the mountains of potatoes and hillocks of bread'.

The quarter deck was set apart for the exclusive use of the 50 unmarried women and 'from them came peal after peal of laughter, song, chorus and hymn. They had been on board long enough to feel at home. Some plied with the busy knitting needle, some read novels, or scanned religious books . . . many leant lazily over

The Ramsey, *at Gravesend in 1871.* (National Maritime Museum).

the bulwarks and chatted and laughed as if the world had no cares and the sea no terrors'.

The reporter, who obviously travelled with the ship down the Thames to the coast, also had an eye for a goodlooking lass as he goes on:

'There were several strapping and comely young women amongst them, and should they, safe and sound, reach the bachelor ridden colony for which they are bound, their fate may be easily predicted without recourse to the black art'.

There was a rigid rule on board ship that, for the entire length of the voyage, the single girls and single men should be kept well and truly apart and directly after the ship began to move, the Captain ordered every male emigrant off the quarter deck and furthermore, announced his intention of clapping in irons the first intruder that breached the rule. These youngsters had many eyes watching them – from the doctor, who considered himself not only the guardian of their physical condition but also of their moral welfare, to the stern Matron – and even the Captain's wife offered to keep her beady eyes upon them. Just to make doubly sure, strong gratings, which were padlocked, effectually shut off one end of the ship from the other.

All this upset the young people considerably and the report goes on: 'One buxom damsel vigorously assured us that she would have married her Ned a week ago had she known of this cruel regulation and she enquired if we couldn't stop the ship and marry them at Gravesend'.

The writer moved around the ship and particularly noted 'a curly-headed urchin, whimsically clad in a smock-frock and highblows, though he could not be seven years of age, pined after his doe rabbit, but his parents certainly did not long after the flesh pots of the Egypt they had forsaken. Mr Richardson introduced us to a sensible-looking and sensible-talking man, who is head of a family of sixteen children, eleven of whom, decently clad and well-fed, were on board, going with him to the land of promise'.

The reporter walked from stem to stern and 'got before the mast among the single men; youth after youth, wearing the blue ribbon of the Union, stepped forward and detailed how their livelihood of five, six and seven shillings a week was suddenly taken from them because they had dared to join the obnoxious association'.

But now they did not care; they were happy to be setting sail aboard a ship that was just bursting with chatter, laughter and excitement.

But who was the 'melancholy brunette leaning over the bulwarks disconsolate, and everyone took notice of her, because she was the one conspicuous exception. Still she refused to be comforted, and kept aloof from her fellow-passengers, brooding over the water as the ship glided through it'. What was her story? Who had she left behind?

The ship passed the Plumstead marshes where the artillery were practising, and a weary-faced woman apologised for the screams of her children 'on the grounds that they never in their lives before heard a big gun'.

The report really captured the atmosphere on board as it continued:

'The sailors running aloft, the friendly greetings of the small craft crossing our track, and the wonders of the Thames, kept young and old fully occupied. A bugle was by-and-by added to the violin, and there was no more touching scene than an assemblage of able-bodied men on the fore-deck, surrounding Mr Richardson who stood on the capstan, and led them off in "God Bless the National Union". The performance was really excellent; a young man who was afterwards stated to be a shepherd, taking the bass part with great accuracy'.

The report concludes 'Even as the summer beauty of the first day may by-and-by be succeeded by storms, the friendly relations and universal happiness visible on every hand may change to unpleasantness, but on Wednesday, the *Ramsey* was the home of a united and cheerful family; and as the few friends who sailed so far left her at Greenhithe, where she made a brief pause to adjust her compasses, bright eyes watched their progress, and merry voices shouted "Goodbye".'

According to the ship's captain, it was an uneventful

voyage. At one point the ship was in the 'doldrums' for three days, but after rounding the Cape of Good Hope, she made 230 miles per day. The passengers kept in good health, though four children under two years of age died en route and there were four births. The good fellowship and harmony remained for the entire voyage, although many of the Bucks workers were seasick, a fact which was mentioned in the song composed during the voyage entitled 'The Ramsey Song'.

'The Channel passed and Lizard Point,
Dear Old England out of sight,
And tossing down rough Biscay Bay,
Our stomach pumps toss'd up all day.
Oh, was not that a jolly spree,
Out upon the wide, wide sea;
To lay upon the deck and cry,
"I'm seasick" on the Ramsey.'

The Captain may have thought it an uneventful voyage but at least one passenger thought otherwise. He wrote home to the effect that from the Cape to the coast of New South Wales '. . . the sea was tremendous. One night in particular it was terrible. A tremendous wave dashed over amidship, and carried part of the bulwark away, and the jib and the top-sails were also taken away; the water came down the hatches into the lower deck, swamping some in their beds. But still we were assured there was no danger'. In fact, the boatswain assured him 'If it was no worse than this, old women would come to sea'.

Cheers racked the *Ramsey* as she dropped anchor in Moreton Bay. Next morning a steamer came to take the emigrants twenty miles up river to Brisbane. Just to see dry land seemed like heaven and 'to see the orange groves and banana plantations, the cotton and sugar fields, the pineapples, and water melons growing around the houses, was beautiful'.

At Brisbane, they were housed in accommodation provided by the Queensland Government and fed liberally until they found work and settled in. They had made it! They were ready and willing to start their new life so far away from the Buckinghamshire countryside.

Richardson was back in Bucks by October of the same year and at a meeting held in Aylesbury Market Square on 9th October, he was able to tell his audience of the successful trip of the *Ramsey* and deliver letters from the emigrants to their relations.

He took yet another group of Buckinghamshire labourers to Queensland in September 1874. This time the ship was the larger 2,000 tons *Indus*; she carried 586 emigrants, among them 197 from Bucks. And although he intended to return, it was not to be. He set out for Tasmania where he had various jobs and adventures until, on 4th May 1878, when the whaleboat on which he was crossing Macquarie Harbour succumbed to a sudden squall, he was drowned at the age of 29.

# Homicide at Hanslope

★

Primrose wine can have a very strange effect on some people. It did on William Farrow, head gamekeeper in the employ of Squire Watts of Hanslope, whose family had been landowners there for centuries.

It was 1912, and the summer turned out to be warm and pleasant with temperatures rising into the nineties. The morning of the 21st July was no exception and, to the sound of distant bells, the Squire and his wife left the manor house as they did regularly every Sunday to attend morning service at Hanslope Church, about a mile and a half away. Nothing untoward happened as they passed through the lodge gates and walked at a steady pace along the road – nor did it during the service.

Squire Edward Hanslope Watts was one of the largest landowners in the County. He was Chairman of the Bench of Magistrates at Stony Stratford, a prominent politician and was said to be held in high regard by his tenants and the people of Hanslope. In the church he sat in the same pew, used by his forebears for generations, directly over the family vault. Little did he know that by the same time the following week he would have joined them. His wife sat with the choir, of which she was a keen member.

The sun streamed through the tall church windows and, after the service, the congregation emerged into the churchyard, the Watts chatting among them before making their way back along the road to their home,

Mrs Watts walking a few yards behind. It was not uncommon in those days for a wife to walk behind her husband, though for a Squire and his wife to do so may seem a bit unusual.

The warm weather did not encourage strenuous exercise and so they were walking at a leisurely pace when they met their old friend Dr Rutherford on his cycle, who stopped for a chat before remounting and moving on.

The tiny procession of two recommenced its journey and all was well with the world as the couple approached the lodge gates, when suddenly a shot rang out from a spinney by the side of the road. Instantly, Squire Watts, shot in the back of the head, pitched to the ground. Mrs Watts, heedless of any danger to herself, rushed to his assistance and as she did so, she caught sight of a man's face peering through the bushes of the spinney. She recognised him as William Farrow, a keeper on their estate. He was half hidden in the trees with his gun still at his shoulder.

'He's firing again' shouted Mrs Watts, dropping by the side of her husband's body, by which action she probably avoided the second shot which could have been meant for her.

Mrs Green, the lodge-keeper's wife, going happily about her work, heard the shot and looked out of the window. To her horror, she perceived the Squire lying in the road, his wife holding him. Mrs Green rushed to the scene and, on her arrival, it was obvious that the Squire was dead. The second shot had hit Squire Watts in the back, tearing his clothes to shreds. So intense had been the shock to Mrs Watts that she fell into a state of complete prostration.

George Green, the coachman, was next on the scene. As he arrived, he heard a third shot coming from the midst of the spinney. He launched himself into the thicket and, following a short track some 35 yards, came across the body of Gamekeeper Farrow, who was lying on the ground with the muzzle of his shot gun close to his face. His head was shattered and death must have been instantaneous.

At this point, Hanslope's one and only law officer, Police Constable Cooper, arrived from the village on his bicycle, having been informed that something terrible had happened to the Squire. It took him a little time to realise the Squire was dead, and he took out his notebook. Most of the villagers at Hanslope were law-abiding and the Constable had only been called upon to deal with trivialities in the way of misdemeanours – such as riding a bicycle without a lamp and so on. To come face to face with murder shook him rigid – here was fame suddenly thrust upon him. Nevertheless he rose to the occasion with efficiency and, at that very moment, he heard Green shout 'I've got 'im'. Entering the spinney he soon found the coachman standing over the body of the Squire's gamekeeper. For a moment he thought he had two murders to deal with, until told the story. He collected the gun and cartridges and licked his pencil just as Dr Rutherford returned to examine the bodies. They carried the body of Edward Hanslope Watts back into his manor house.

Now what had turned William Farrow, hitherto as far as was known, a peaceful man, into a murderer? A shocked countryside was convinced that primrose wine had something to do with it.

The *Wolverton Express* of 26th July reported that at the inquest on the two bodies, held the day after the murder at The Greyhound Inn, Tathall End, Farrow's wife wept copiously. She said her husband would have celebrated his 46th birthday the following day. She also

71

said that on that fateful Sunday he had left home at around 10.30 am, taking some cartridges but no gun. He had told her the cartridges were for Mr Whitbread, a tenant on the estate. Prior to leaving home, he took his game book out and made an entry. She identified her husband's writing but added she did not suppose he would write very steadily in the state he was in at the time.

'Had he been drinking then?' asked the Coroner. The tears flowed even more copiously. 'Yes' was the answer, 'a whole jug of primrose wine'. There was an audible 'Ah' from the well of the court.

Farrow's next port of call, after leaving home that Sunday morning, was on Mrs Beasley of Manor Farm where he asked for a glass of beer to quench his thirst. Mrs Beasley stated in dramatic tones that she had not liked the look of the man. His eyes were glassy and he did not look natural. Her husband's gun had been by the door and Farrow commenced to fiddle with it, which had the effect of producing a half pint of beer with rapidity. He then asked for a razor before the people came out of church. 'What?' exclaimed Mrs Beasley in fright. He said his own razor was being ground, and then, to her intense relief, he turned away and she saw him no more.

Henry Martin, under-keeper at Hanslope Park, gave evidence that he had seen Farrow on the Saturday night before the tragedy when he had appeared completely normal to him. He told the court that it had been a hard and fast rule of the late Squire that no keeper or other employee of his should carry a gun on a Sunday, which would explain the fact that Farrow had hidden his gun, the murder weapon, in the spinney on the day before the tragic event. Martin held the court's undivided attention when he revealed that Farrow had been under

*William Farrow, Head Gamekeeper at Hanslope Park.*

notice to leave the employ of Squire Watts – what for, Martin did not know – and he emphasised that he had never heard Farrow say a word against the Squire though he had mentioned at one time 'lies' being told about him.

Mrs Farrow said that she was completely unaware that her husband had been under notice and she confirmed that never once had he said anything detrimental about his master in her presence.

Constable Cooper was then called and he moistened

73

his finger to leaf through his notebook to the appropriate page. He recounted with aplomb the happenings of that fateful morning in precise order.

Dr Underwood said that the gamekeeper had suffered a bout of sunstroke the previous summer whilst out on a shoot and had had to be brought home on a stretcher. He added that sunstroke could induce a sudden apoplectic seizure. But the court felt that for this to take place a year later, and when the man had been perfectly alright in the interim, was a bit much to credit.

The jury returned a verdict of wilful murder against Farrow in respect of the death of Squire Watts and *felo de se* in regard to his own death. They gave no qualification whatsoever as to the state of Farrow's mind and consequently, by their verdict, judged him to have been sane at the time of the murder.

People were left puzzled. Why had Farrow been given notice by the Squire after working for him for two years without seemingly giving any reason for dissatisfaction? The reason was never established and no-one seemed to know. Gossip was rife. Some said it was because the Squire had wished to reduce his staff of two gamekeepers to one. But if this was so, why dismiss the senior keeper, a man with a wife and children, and not the junior?

Gradually yet another theory evolved. It transpired that earlier in the year both the Squire and his wife had gone abroad for a few weeks and Mrs Watts had asked Farrow to look after her favourite dog whilst she was away. On her return she was horrified and not a little annoyed to find that the dog had died through sheer neglect on the part of Farrow and she called him 'murderer'. Prophetic to say the least, and a good enough reason for her husband to dismiss the keeper to please his wife. This could also account for Farrow muttering about 'lies'.

But, who knows, perhaps Farrow, inflamed by primrose wine, intended to kill the lady and not the Squire, or even both!

All this happened over 80 years ago and, if any kind of lesson is to emerge over the years, perhaps it is 'Go easy on the primrose wine'.

# Fires at Olney

★

It seems that the town of Olney suffered more than its fair share of fires in the last century. The disaster of 1854, which was called by the press 'The Great Fire of Olney', was not the first or the last bad fire the town and its people were to endure. As the *Northampton Herald* reported at the time 'often during the last few years we have had to record the destruction of life and property by fire in this little town.' And the *Illustrated London News* remarked 'A sort of fatality appears to attend the town.'

The first record of a fire was written by the poet, William Cowper, distinguished resident in the town. This took place in 1777 when seven or eight cottages went up in smoke and, had not the wind suddenly changed, half the town would undoubtedly have been destroyed.

Cowper wrote again of a fire that took place in November 1783. He described people screaming up his staircase and of being called from his bed by the cry of 'fire!' He peered from his window to see fires raging in three places in the town. This time it was thought to have been 'maliciously started'. To quote Cowper: 'A tar barrel and a quantity of tallow had made a tremendous blaze and the appearance every moment became more formidable'.

Thankfully this time there was no wind. The night

was so calm that candles without lanterns burned outside in the street as steadily as if they had been indoors. People in fear of fire reaching their houses removed as fast as they could all their possessions to the house of some neighbour which was thought to be more secure. Cowper went on to say that in the space of two hours his own house was so filled with all sorts of lumber that 'there was not even room for a chair by the fireside.'

Outside, the street was filled with people running hither and thither through the smoke. Chaos reigned and much looting took place including drunkenness and riot. 'Everything was stolen that could be got at and every drop of liquor drunk that was not guarded'. Such was the turmoil that poor George Griggs in his panic gave eighteen guineas to a woman who, in his hurry, he mistook for his wife. Needless to say she was never seen again; neither was his money.

In spite of this dreadful scene of conflagration and wild lawlessness, there was not so much damage as at

RUINS OF OLNEY, AFTER THE RECENT FIRE.

first envisaged. No lives were lost and no limbs broken.

Inevitably with the dawn came retribution and justice for lawbreakers, such as Sue Rivis for stealing a piece of beef which she fervently swore she had only been looking after for someone else; and other women who had filled their aprons with anything they could lay their hands on.

One young man, convicted of stealing, was sentenced to be whipped at the cart's tail from the 'stone house' to the 'High Arch' and back. This provided an amusing scene as the Beadle, whose job it was to carry out the beating, must have had a soft spot for the miscreant, as he filled his left hand with red ochre. After every stroke he drew the lash of the whip through this hand so that when he struck the culprit, it gave the appearance of a wound upon the skin, whereas it was done in such a way as to cause no pain.

But the Constable spotted this trick and launched himself upon the Beadle with his cane, bellowing at him to strike harder. Still the Beadle would not do so and thus the procession progressed with the Beadle supposedly lashing his victim and the Constable following behind caning the Beadle. Then a young strapping lass could bear it no longer and grabbed the Constable, spinning him round and slapping his face with 'Amazonian fury'.

Six years later in 1786, yet another disastrous fire consumed 43 houses. Then in 1853, fireraisers were at work filling the people with fear. Any moving shadow on a dark night could be someone intent upon arson.

First, attempts were made on farms. On one a cowhouse was destroyed and the *Northampton Herald* reported 'The cries and bellowing of the animals was frightful'. This was followed by the firing of the barn of a local Vet.

It was on a Tuesday evening that the 'incendiaries' were successful in firing the premises of the Baker, the flames quickly spreading to a watch factory. Two men, John Marson and William Scott, in attempting to rescue property, were killed by the collapse of a building and Jacob Clifton died a painful death of burns a few weeks later. Said the *Bucks Herald* 'The destruction of property is great and much excitement prevails in the town and neighbourhood'.

At this time the town consisted of many thatched cottages and buildings with small factories and shops with storehouses in the gardens, and courtyards of small workshops.

On 26th June 1854, around two o'clock in the afternoon, began the worst fire in the history of Olney. It was discovered that the thatch of a small wash-house to the rear of Daniel Morgan's, the Grocer, situated about the middle of the High Street on the western side, was alight. The flames rapidly spread to the premises of Buchell, the Dyers, next door. A boisterous wind carried the burning thatch in a north-easterly direction and, before any kind of warning could be given, the premises of Covington, the Blacksmith, lower down on the other side of the street, were ablaze. More and more strands of burning thatch were taken up by the wind carrying them from house to house until dwellings, outbuildings, barns and two or three farmyards were enveloped in smoke and flames.

The three parish 'engines', assisted by two from Newport Pagnell and one from Yardley Hastings, worked feverishly side by side to no avail. The fire 'engine' of those days consisted of a fire cart with manual pump and water was taken from a nearby river or pond.

*The 'Great Fire' in Olney High Street, 26 June 1854 and (inset) the fire at Olney Mill in January 1878.*

The fire relentlessly made its way from ridge to ridge until some thirty houses on the eastern side and some ten or twelve opposite, together with outbuildings, were raging infernos. Ladders placed against the buildings in order to remove property were instantly consumed by tongues of fire. Once again, many people seeing the fire moving ever closer to their homes removed their goods and furniture to places thought to be a safe distance away, but this time the fire was travelling at so fast a pace, their goods were destroyed before they realised they were in danger a second time. Jonathan Field, the Tailor, having removed his property to the house of a friend, was forced to watch the friend's house razed to the ground.

80

In all, the number of houses destroyed was 55 and 25 damaged, making a total of 80 – just one sixth of the total number of houses in the town. There was also great loss of stores; hay and beans, etc.

More than 300 persons were made homeless, losing all their worldly possessions. Some were housed in the National School, some in the cottages of their kind neighbours and some were forced to live in the open. The loss was estimated at between £9,000 and £10,000 but insurance extended to only £3,000. It was decided that the fire had been accidental and had broken out near enough at the same spot as the fire of 1786.

The *Bucks Herald* of 1st July 1854 contained a notice describing the 'terrible fire at Olney' and stating that an appeal committee had been formed with the Vicar, the Rev Dr Langley, as Chairman together with a sub-committee of ladies who, it was doubtless felt, would be more conversant with the needs of the homeless. The Vicar earnestly appealed to the 'benevolent to make contributions for the relief of those suffering' and listed various banks where these could be made. The response must have been good for by 12th July there appeared in the *Bucks Herald* a letter from the Vicar thanking all those that had made such generous donations.

The *Illustrated London News* printed sketches showing the activity that took place both whilst the fire was raging and the aftermath; the utter desolation with blackened chimneys and gables standing stark against the skyline. Yet 'the calamity was borne with patience and resignation, such as could not help but excite the sympathy of every Christian community'.

Around 1876, a man called Charles Henry Whitworth purchased Olney Mill and then proceeded to improve it, laying out several thousand pounds, which enabled him to run a very much more extensive business. On Thursday night, 3rd January 1878, an alarm of 'fire!' was raised in the town. The townspeople streamed in the direction of the Church, but it was not that building ablaze – it was the Mill – much to the extreme agitation of Mr Whitworth. The Olney Engine arrived promptly but there was little their inadequate equipment could do against the fury of such flames, which soon caught the contents of the top floors and leaped so high they could be seen for several miles around. Plenty of willing helpers removed a number of corn sacks from the lower floors, but falling timbers soon made this task too dangerous. Soon after, the wooden lift caught fire and it was said that although the scene of the burning Mill was terrible to behold at this time, it was also considered beautiful with flames pouring through every crack and crevice, whilst the reflection upon the Church showed up the stone spire against the dark sky.

The flames began to spread very close to the house adjoining the Mill and the men of the Olney Engine played water on it to keep it damp whilst others removed any valuables.

The Newport Pagnell Engine then arrived on the scene 'whose panting steeds betokened the rate at which they had travelled' and immediately commenced to work and, although it looked impossible, it was entirely due to the struggles of the men from Newport Pagnell that the house was saved.

It took many hours to master the flames and the engines did not leave the scene until half past eight the next morning. The gutted Mill presented a sorry picture – a black, charred mass.

This disaster appeared to be the last straw! The leaders of the community, besieged by the people, held a meeting at which they formed a committee to raise funds in order to furnish the town with a full blown Fire Brigade. The response was instantaneous, local landowners leading the way with generous donations and town traders only too willing to chip in. The result was that eight months after that first meeting, the Olney Fire Brigade was formed consisting of a dozen volunteer members who gave freely of their time and even bought their own uniforms, and a further sixteen members who were paid for their time excluding practices and assemblies. A set of rules was drawn up which members were expected to firmly keep. One was that on 'hearing the call each member should proceed to the Engine house and report'. Any member failing to do so was fined the astronomical sum of ten shillings!

The new Olney Fire Brigade under Captain Booth proved to be the pride of the town and the people felt safer because of its existence. When in November 1882 the alarm was given that a large carpenter's shop was alight, the Brigade was on the spot at once. They instantly set to work with a will, but once again the wind was high, and the contents of the building were highly combustible, making their splendid efforts useless. However, they did keep the fire in check by saturating all the neighbouring buildings.

Whilst this was happening, a portion of other premises caught alight. As the fire reached the lower storeys, the blaze increased. The flames then attacked a wooden building filled with furniture, but due to the skill of the Brigade all was saved, together with thatched buildings in close proximity. There were times when the fire, having subsided, suddenly shot up again. Nevertheless, the Brigade persevered; playing water on the smouldering mass until all trace of fire was quite extinguished. The origin of this conflagration was unknown.

In 1887, some cottages situated in The Leys caught fire. At the time, the Baptist Chapel was packed to capacity with a large congregation when some 'thoughtless person' poked his head in the door and shouted 'fire!' Panic reigned, and had it not been for the coolness and presence of mind of the pastor, it was thought many could have lost their lives in the stampede for the door. The Fire Brigade rushed to The Leys but unfortunately could not overcome the blaze until three cottages had been destroyed.

There were other smaller fires which did not bear lengthy reports in the local press. In the present century there were at least three memorable ones. In 1928 the Cowley Boot and Shoe Factory was gutted, as was the Cowper Memorial Congregational Church in 1965. And in that year also the Olney Mill was once again destroyed.

All these trials and tribulations the people of Olney bore with remarkable forbearance, courage and fortitude, always helping one another.

Perhaps the philosophy of the people is best described in the ballads and poems written by locals after the Great Fire of 1854. Copies of these were sold in aid of the homeless and reveal a kind of faith and resignation:

'These fires were bad, we know full well,
But naught to that which burns;
Where sinners go, in dismal hell,
From whence they ne're return.

May these calamities be blessed
And prove a lasting good;
Surely they will, to those possessed
With sincere love to God.'

# The Daredevil Flyer from Dunsmore

★

A startling and unusual story appeared in the *Daily Express* on the morning of 9th February 1962, and on 23rd February, the *Bucks Herald* headlined 'LOCAL MAN'S PETRIFIED BODY FOUND AFTER 29 YEARS.'

It told the story of a French Army Patrol that had come across the wrecked plane and body of a pilot in that part of the Sahara Desert called by local Bedouin tribes 'The Land of Thirst' – the very core of the Sahara, trackless and waterless. The body was lying on its side and in such a remarkable state of preservation that a scar on the forehead, which had obviously been received in the crash, was easily discernible. Parts exposed to the air had become mummified and were like parchment – part was covered by a thin layer of sand. It was apparent the unfortunate flyer had sheltered from the merciless sun under the wing of his plane and with foresight had strapped on the fuselage a waterproof envelope containing his log book, passport etc. On some blank pages in his log book the dead man had kept a diary of the eight days it had taken him to die of thirst, and revealing that the crash had occurred in April 1933. The flight had left England on 11th April bound for South Africa. It had been intended to break the record held by Amy Johnson who a few

*The wreckage of* Southern Cross Minor, *with Lancaster's partly buried skeleton in the foreground.*

months earlier had made the flight in four days, six hours and fifty-four minutes.

The plane, a light aircraft, was an Avro Avian named *Southern Cross Minor*. After perusing all the documents, the French Patrol knew they were looking down at a body that had lain in the middle of the desert for 29 years and that it was all that remained of Captain William Newton Lancaster who had lived at Dunsmore, near Wendover and later at Monks Risborough, Buckinghamshire.

Captain Bill Lancaster had been a keen airman with many flights behind him and had proved himself to be a courageous, though reckless flyer. Born in 1898, the son of an electrical engineer, he had lived a chequered life, full of adventure and daring exploits in many fields. In his teens he had been sent to Australia where he worked on a sheep station, and at the age of eighteen he joined the Australian Cavalry where he became an accomplished horseman. But Europe was in the throes of the First World War and he sought a chance to return to England. He transferred to the

Australian Air Force. In no time he was a fully trained pilot and commissioned as a second lieutenant in November 1917, flying on operations.

In 1918 he received a commission in the Royal Air Force and was posted to India. By this time, he had married and his eldest daughter was born in that country. In 1923 he was posted back to England at Halton, near Wendover.

The manor house and vast estates of Halton had once belonged to Alfred de Rothschild who had allowed a great proportion of his lands to be used by the Army and the Royal Flying Corps during the First World War. Upon his death, the Royal Air Force had taken over the whole of the estate. It eventually became an important training base and airfield.

Bill Lancaster was happy at Halton. He flew regularly from the airfield and appreciated this lovely part of the Chilterns where the hills reached their highest point. He purchased a house at Dunsmore for his wife and daughter. His personality widened and he enjoyed the company of the men, though he was not particularly popular with them. They thought he was something of a 'big-head', always boasting, and as far as they were concerned this was proved in 1924 when an International Rodeo was staged at Wembley Stadium, scheduled to last three weeks. It was announced in all the newspapers that roping, steering and riding competitions were to be organised, not the least being the open challenge to anyone who felt so inclined to stay on a bucking bronco for two minutes. The challenge was taken up by expert horsemen from America, Australia and Canada. The first time the competition was held all five competitors suffered injuries, some serious. *The Times* stated: 'Any man who can sit such an animal must have the qualities of a limpet.'

When this was read aloud in the mess at Halton, Lancaster boasted he could do it. His fellow airmen encouraged him, quite convinced he would be thrown immediately, and what is more they looked forward to seeing it happen.

They were disappointed. He did it! The gyrations of the horse were dreadful to behold, but it could not detach Bill Lancaster who, it was said, performed the ride in a bowler hat and pin-stripe suit.

Local man Fred Hibberd was in charge of the power station at Halton. He had been a member of the Royal Flying Corps and was a clever engineer. Lancaster, who knew his commission was due to expire in 1925, looked around in good time for some business or trade. Together with Fred Hibberd he decided to set up a bus and taxi service in Wendover, persuading his father to invest some of his surplus funds. After a visit and approval by father, the new business began trading under the name of the Red Rose Garage, a play on the name Lancaster. This garage, under the same name, is there to this day.

It was in 1925 that the RAF decided to use parachutes for the first time. It had previously been thought by them that if a man was given a parachute, he would be less likely to try to save his plane if it got into difficulties. Volunteers were called for to go on a parachute training course at Henlow. Needless to say, Bill Lancaster was one of the first to volunteer and it was decided that, at the Hendon Air Display, three men would jump from respective planes. This was not an easy feat, as the man was required to climb from his rear cockpit down a ladder which reached to the base of the fuselage. The pilot then signalled when he was to jump. Bill Lancaster was the second man to do so.

Life was now pretty good for Lancaster, but he had always wanted to gain distinction as an aeronaut. He desperately wanted to make a solo flight that would become headline news and make him famous. At his home in the village of Dunsmore, he started to think about a solo flight to Australia, planning the route and the best plane for the job. It was around this time at a party that he met 'Chubbie'. She was to have a profound effect on his life.

Australian Mrs 'Chubbie' Miller was twenty-five, dark, petite, and married to a journalist. She was not particularly good-looking but possessed a vivacious personality and a thirst for adventure. Her marriage had been on the rocks for some time and she had only been in England a matter of months. Lancaster began to tell her of his proposed flight to Australia and she came up with an idea which rather stunned him. She asked that, provided she could acquire the necessary promotional finance, he should take her with him. She managed to acquire the necessary backing, and as this would be the first such flight carrying a passenger, the press began to take an interest. The result was that at 2.40 pm on the afternoon of 14th October 1927, Lancaster and Chubbie took off from Lympne en route for Port Darwin, Australia in a two seater Avro Avian aircraft named, not surprisingly, the Red Rose.

It was on this flight that Lancaster first proved his wanton disregard for expert advice. Many things went wrong. To start with, on that first leg of the journey he landed in a field two miles short of the airfield at Abbeyfield in France and, because the space was too small to take off with a full load, he left Chubbie behind to walk the two miles to the airfield! Once over the desert, they ran into sandstorms and were shot at by tribesmen. All other aircraft were grounded due to heavy floods at Hinaidi, but Lancaster took off through the flood waters.

At Basra, the RAF strongly advised him not to cross the Persian Gulf but instead to follow the coast around to the next stop. But the impatient Lancaster would have none of it – it would take longer – so they headed out directly across the Gulf. The magneto began to give trouble and the engine began to cough and stutter. They looked down into the waters below to see literally dozens of sharks. Chubbie was later to say she had never known such fear. Lancaster nursed the plane along and they were exhausted when they reached Bushire. They arrived at Calcutta on December 19th. By now Lancaster had taught Chubbie to fly and, after they had taken off on the next leg of their journey, there was a nasty moment when her control stick jammed, and they hurtled towards the ground. A last minute wrench saved them. Over Rangoon, the engine packed up but Lancaster was able to make a smooth forced landing in some rice fields. This time it took ten days for the plane to be repaired, and although Lancaster was repeatedly warned that there was a glut of snakes in the area and to keep all apertures on the plane closed whilst it was on the ground, he paid no heed. Consequently, when they were airborne once more on the next lap of their journey, Chubbie was panic stricken to find a snake wriggling at the bottom of her cockpit. Gritting her teeth, she killed it with the control stick – of all things!

The two flyers landed at Singapore and were fêted. The last stretch of the flight now lay before them – 2,500 miles to Port Darwin. Once again they took off and reached 150 feet when, for some unknown reason at the time, the engine completely cut out and they crashed. Chubbie managed to walk away from the plane, but Lancaster was unconscious and they were both taken to the local Hospital. When Lancaster examined the plane afterwards, he found that it was a stoppage in the fuel supply that had caused the engine to cut out and this was entirely due to the fact that he himself had neglected to set his fuel switches before take off – they were still in the 'off' position!

The Red Rose was duly patched up and, after flying across Java and Sumatra, landed on the island of Timor. They were now only 500 miles from their goal and facing the longest sea crossing of the entire flight. There was yet another delay due to a spongy airfield caused by heavy rain, and they actually took off on March 19th. It was not long before they and the plane were engulfed in torrential rain. Neither of them had ever seen anything like it. Visibility was practically nil and the engine began to stutter and pop. Lancaster struggled to maintain height, but he dropped rapidly – the engine sprang to life and up they climbed, only to lose height again as the engine once more began misfiring. This was repeated time and again – it was like riding on a terrifying switchback. Travelling many miles in this manner, they eventually sighted Port Darwin.

They landed a bedraggled, exhausted pair, to find the welcoming committee, tired of waiting, had long since gone home. But all the many dangers and disappointments the two had shared had brought them close together and by now they were very much in love. They had established two records: the Red Rose was the first aeroplane to take a woman to Australia and the first light plane to take two people there. Its manufacturers did very well out of the publicity.

Bill Lancaster and his Chubbie went to America, where he made a good living from flying and Chubbie, after completing her training as a pilot, entered air races. Both became well-known as a dashing, adventurous couple. They rented a house in Miami and became friendly with a good-looking, charming young writer with a weakness for drink. His name was Haden Clarke. Chubbie had long wanted her life story written and she chose Haden to ghost-write it. Whilst Lancaster was on a flight to the west coast, she wrote to tell him she had fallen in love with Haden. This was the greatest blow Lancaster had received in his life for he adored his Chubbie and he had regarded Haden as his friend. He hastily flew back to the house in Miami where they told him they wished to marry. The three of them discussed the matter till the early hours of the morning. Eventually they all went to bed, the two men sleeping in single beds in a porch room.

Chubbie was awakened by Lancaster banging on her door saying that Haden had shot himself in the head whilst in bed. The gun he had used belonged to Lancaster, who now presented her with two suicide notes – one addressed to himself and the other to Chubbie. Haden died later in hospital. The suicide notes were thoroughly examined, found to be false and Lancaster admitted having written them himself, and even trying to coax the dying Haden to sign them. He was arrested and charged with murder. The trial lasted sixteen days with both he and Chubbie taking the stand. However, in the end it was concluded that Haden *had* committed suicide and Lancaster was acquitted.

The chastened couple returned to England but did not live together. Lancaster found it now incredibly difficult to obtain a job flying and came to the conclusion that another ambitious flight was necessary in order to bring his name to the fore. He determined to beat Amy Johnson's record from England to South Africa, and this time his father agreed to finance the

*Lancaster with* Southern Cross Minor.

trip. Lancaster made his preparations. As he would be flying alone, it seemed to him that the most suitable aircraft available was a later model of the Avro Avian, the cruising speed of which was 95 miles per hour, 20 miles slower than Amy Johnson's plane, but Lancaster thought that if he succeeded with such a handicap it would be considered even more creditable. He felt sure he could do it by allowing himself practically no rest.

The route he planned followed closely that taken by Amy. He proposed to take off from Lympne, fly across France, the Pyrenees and the Mediterranean to Oran in Algeria. The first leg would take place in daylight, but the difficulty was that he planned another short re-fuelling stop at Reggan and this meant he would have to fly from Oran to Reggan after nightfall as he could not afford to rest. Furthermore Reggan would be difficult to find at night and, if he were to miss it, the vast Sahara lay beyond. Then, on from Reggan, across the Sahara to Nigeria and direct to Cape Lopez cutting a few hours off Amy Johnson's time. He would still be

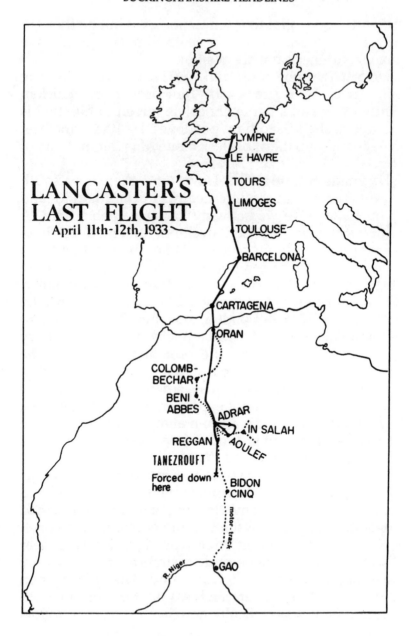

# LANCASTER'S
# LAST FLIGHT
### April 11th-12th, 1933

LYMPNE
LE HAVRE
TOURS
LIMOGES
TOULOUSE
BARCELONA
CARTAGENA
ORAN
COLOMB-BECHAR
BENI ABBES
ADRAR
IN SALAH
AOULEF
REGGAN
TANEZROUFT
Forced down here
BIDON CINQ
motor-track
R. Niger
GAO

left with 2,500 miles to reach Cape Town but he thought with the African coastline beneath him, he would have a constant check on his position.

He left Lympne after dark on 11th April 1933. The only food he carried with him was some chicken sandwiches and a bar of chocolate, given to him by his mother as she kissed him 'goodbye'. He had some beef extract and two thermos flasks, one of water and one of coffee.

He made a stop at Le Havre and then flew south across France, but ran into headwinds and had to land at Barcelona. He was already losing valuable time. A pilot who met him at Barcelona remarked on how fraught and tense he seemed. When he reached Oran it had taken him fifteen hours – Amy Johnson had only taken twelve. Here also he faced an added difficulty. The authorities had no knowledge of the insurance he had effected back in London, and they flatly refused to let him take off until they either had the necessary confirmation or he paid the premium again. This he could not do, so he signed a statement to the effect that he was flying entirely at his own risk and that, if he went missing, he did not expect anyone to set out on a rescue operation. He was then allowed to proceed, but he had by then been grounded for six hours – Amy had taken only four.

The journey to Reggan did not prove to be as easy as he had thought. He flew into a sandstorm, blundered off course and took some time to regain it. After he had landed at Reggan, the sandstorm became much worse. Officials there advised him to rest as he was near distraction with fatigue and frustration. He took only three hours to rest and refused food. The officials then told him it was sheer madness to take off in such conditions. It was difficult enough, they said, to follow the motor track to Gao in daylight, let alone in darkness, especially as he had no lighting on his instrument panel for steering a compass course. Lancaster's reply was that he could manage with some matches. They lent him a torch and he made a very bad take off and was seen no more – that is until February 1962!

His diary told of his last hours – how he had been flying the compass course, which meant he had lost sight of the motor track as had been predicted. There was no moon and it was pitch dark. He crashed upside down and found only his head and nose were cut. He considered himself lucky. 'I have just escaped the most unpleasant death.'

And there he lay, under the wing of his plane, *The Southern Cross Minor*, for eight days, longing for water and a rescue party to find him. Certainly they searched for him – parties went along the track from Reggan and also from Gao. Planes scanned the glaring sands to no avail. He sent messages to all his loved ones, and typical of the marvellous flyers of those days, he signed off: 'The chin is up right to the end.'

# The Great
# Train Robbery

★

Whoever would have thought that the small, peaceful village of Cheddington would one day leap into the world's headlines as it did in August 1963? For on the 8th of that month, one of the most audacious train robberies ever committed took place at Sears Crossing, slightly to the north of the village.

Planned as meticulously as a military campaign, the robbers successfully got away with £2.5 million in used bank notes — at least for a time!

The crooks had received a tip-off that at a certain time the mail train from London to Glasgow would be passing through Sears Crossing carrying up to £5 million in used notes in the second coach behind the engine. It was usual that this coach should contain the 'High Value Packets'; the third coach carried the sorters.

The plan was to fix the signals at Sears Crossing so that the train would be forced to a stop. The next step was to sever the connection between the second coach and the remainder of the train — then to drive the engine and the £5 million a few miles further on to a road crossing called Bridego Bridge. Waiting at the foot of the embankment there, disguised as army lorries, were the vehicles in which the robbers could drive away with their booty to a hide-a-way, a remote farm called 'Leatherslade', close to the Oxfordshire border with

*Bridego Bridge, as it is today.*

Bucks.

In order that the operation should be completely successful, they recruited an expert in railway signals and the art of bringing trains to a halt. They also secured a retired train driver to take over from the original one and drive the train on to Bridego Bridge.

At first all went well. The train came to a halt. The fireman alighted from the train and was grabbed. The engine driver then put up a fight and had to be coshed. The old train driver with the robbers proved to be an absolute failure. He could not even start the engine, so the coshed engine driver was propped up to the controls and forced to start the engine.

Every other part of the plan ran smoothly. At Bridego Bridge, the precious sacks of bank notes were swiftly and silently loaded into the waiting vehicles and,

*Police standing guard over the robbed mail van at Euston Station.*

within an hour, the thieves were some twenty miles away at Leatherslade Farm, near Oakley. Here the count began, and the gang went wild when they realised they had lifted over £2.5 million, lighting cigarettes with some of the notes. Ironically, they played 'Monopoly' to while away the time.

Meanwhile, a huge police hunt was underway and had switched from Cheddington to the seaports. Aylesbury became the nerve centre of the hunt where top brass from Scotland Yard gathered, together with

99

practically the entire force of the Bucks Constabulary. Eventually, the vacated Leatherslade Farm was discovered, more or less under their noses, and although the criminals thought they had taken all precautions, finger prints were revealed. This evidence led to the capture of some of the robbers – others were picked up one by one. The so-called 'master mind' managed to elude the police for five years before he was arrested. Those caught at the time were taken back to near the scene of the crime, the little courthouse in the village of Linslade.

The old county town of Aylesbury was the scene of the trial, which opened before Mr Justice Edmund Davies on 20th January 1964, and the impact on the town was tremendous. From the moment the date of the trial became public, hotels and boarding houses were booked to capacity, and, as the date drew near, hoards of people flooded into the town – lawyers, press and police among them. The town creaked with the weight of it all and tradespeople found it an absolute bonanza. The eyes and ears of the world were turned on Aylesbury.

The venue for the trial was the offices of the Rural District Council. The room where many a debate on sewerage had taken place in years past was transformed into an Assize Court with witness box and microphones. A special dock was constructed to hold the twenty accused and their warders. When all was finished, it was said to resemble the courtroom where the famous Nuremberg trials had taken place some years before.

The Chamber and other rooms for the accommodation of witnesses, Counsel, shorthand writers and others, were rented for the sum of £20 per day plus cleaning and other charges. Thirty barristers took part and administrative staff were hard pressed to find room for the many solicitors who briefed them. The world's press clamoured for a place and forty newspaper, radio and television reporters, including foreign newspapers and agencies, crammed into five rows of seats allotted to them at the rear of the court.

The crowds that gathered outside the Council Offices to see the arrival of the prisoners were frustrated. The special van, divided into compartments for each of the accused, drew right up to the door of the building and a cordon of police officers kept back the sightseers, whilst a police dog with a handler kept a watchful eye.

A long, winding queue formed hoping to get into the public gallery. Those that managed to do so found themselves looking down on a sea of white barristers' wigs and local ratepayers among them wondered how much all this was going to cost.

The local historian, anxious to record the proceedings for the annals of the town history, managed to secure a good seat in the body of the court. He had been attending trials for over forty years, but never one like this, and he was determined to see it right through to the bitter end – no matter how long it lasted.

Before this packed and excited court stood the accused – an assortment of big and small names in the criminal world, some well known, some of lesser fame. There were names like Ronald Biggs, the greatest escaper of them all, and whose subsequent South American adventures occupied world headlines for many years afterwards; Charlie Wilson and Roy James, the racing driver known as 'the Weasel'; and there were several women amongst them. All had been cogs in the wheel of the great master plan, some playing larger parts than others. The most serious charge of all was that of armed robbery.

At the opening of the proceedings thirty be-wigged heads bowed to the Judge as he took his seat, and the prosecution reckoned that each member of the gang must have received at least £100,000 from the mail train ambush.

To the Jurors it seemed as if the trial was going to be endless, as there were 613 exhibits to handle and 240 witnesses to be heard. In all it lasted five tedious weeks – the defence did not start until mid-February. On the 14th of that month, the Jury took a coach trip to Aylesbury Prison to examine one of the major exhibits in the case – a Land Rover that had been found at Leatherslade Farm. One of the prison courtyards was turned into a court room for the occasion whilst Judge and Jury examined the same. Eleven of the accused also looked it over and even sat in it.

It was not until mid-March that the Judge commenced his lengthy summing up, and it was at this juncture that a development appeared in the case that excited the press considerably. One of the Jurors reported having been approached by a gentleman (obviously a friend of some of the accused) who offered him money if he would attempt to sway the Jury when the time came. This information caused a furore and the other Jurors immediately asked for Police protection, not only for themselves but also for their families. The Judge granted the same then and there and a twenty-four hour watch was ordered as requested. Police hurriedly interviewed the Juror in the hope of finding and charging the person who attempted the bribe.

On Monday, 23rd March, the Jury left the Court in a bus code-named 'Friday's Child' en route for a secret hideout, and they took all 613 exhibits along with them. Even more members of the world's press crowded into Aylesbury to await the verdict.

The Jury were a grand bunch of people, but unfortunately they did not have a very good time locked away in the secret hideout which later transpired to be the Grange Youth Club in Wendover Way. Here they were 'cooped up' for three nights and two days with no television, radio or newspapers and with all telephones cut off so they could receive no messages. However, there was a record player in their accommodation, but as they were left only 'Rock and Roll' records, they did not think it appropriate to play that kind of music. The strain was hard to bear.

Back in Court on the 51st day of the trial, the Jury said 'Guilty' nineteen times. Sentencing did not take place until a week later, when the press and media 'zoomed' back into Aylesbury. People queued outside the Court in heavy rain from 7 am in the hope of getting in by 10.30 am, plain clothed officers mingling among them. Within just thirty minutes, the Judge had meted out prison sentences totalling 573 years. The terms ranged from three to thirty years, and seven of the robbers received the maximum sentences.

Despite the fact that it had been the greatest train robbery ever, the world gasped at the severity of the sentences. The mother of one of those sentenced made something of a disturbance in court when she shouted out 'What about 'is poor ole Mother, Y'r Honour?' But her son called back as he was led away to the cells 'Don't worry, Mum, I'm still young!' As the lady was evicted from court, her voice becoming fainter, she was heard to say ''Ere keep your hands orf me, I'm seventy three'.

The Judge then turned to the foreman of the Jury and his fellow Jurors and thanked them for their services and the way they had borne 'an almost unbearable burden' for thirty weary weeks. Feeling vastly relieved

# The Bu

No. 6,886    Established 1832    LARGEST CIRCU    FRI

# NOW IT'S JOUR

Ronald Arthur BIGGS
**30 YEARS**

Thomas William WISBEY
**30 YEARS**

Roy John JAMES (The W
**30 YEARS**

Charles Frederick WILSON
**30 YEARS**

Robert WELCH
**30 YEARS**

## Mr. Bacon stole the gammon

A 52-YEAR-OLD man admitted stealing a leg of gammon and a leg of pork, together worth 69s., when he appeared at Great Missenden Magistrates' Court on Monday. He is Leslie James Bacon, of 2, Pankridge Drive, Prestwood.

Bacon admitted stealing the pork and gammon on February 18, from his employers, C. Stevens and Son, of Prestwood.

Inspector W. Brough, prosecuting, told the Bench that Bacon has been employed by the firm for 33 years as a boner.

"He is responsible for checking waste material which is sold to various other firms," he said, and added, "but he has no authority to dispose of any of this material."

The offence came to light when Mr. Albert Archibald W... was seen by police on

He told the police, "I'm sorry, it was a silly thing to do" and made a statement admitting the offence.

**FINED £5**

In the statement he said: "Mr. Willis came to the factory yesterday. I gave him the legs of pork and gammon because I knew he would sell them and give me some of the money."

He told the magistrates: "I am deeply sorry," and was fined £5. It is his first offence.

The case against Willis, of 2, Beavers Lane, Hounslow, Middlesex, who was alleged to have received the meat, was adjourned until May 11, because he was not in court.

## NOW WE ALL KNOW!

Could you direct anyone to Hartwell View, Aylesbury?

Cllr. E. C. Bentley told Aylesbury Borough Council on Monday

## IN 30 MINUTES JUDGE IMPOSES SENTENCES OF 573 YEARS

## "Sordid violenc by gree

SENTENCES totalling 573 years were mete 30 minutes by Mr. Justice Edmund Davie Crown Court, Aylesbury, yesterday morning the closing climax of the 58th day of the Gr Robbery Trial. The sentences on the 12 me dock ranged from three to 30 years.

A crowded courtroom — some people we ing in heavy rain at 7 a.m. for the 10.30 a.m. h heard the Judge describe the robbery as "a sordid violence inspired by vast greed".

Such a grave crime called

armed robbery. "You

104

# Herald

NORTH BUCKS

26 PAGES     Price 3d.

SECOND EDITION

# EY'S END

# JUDGMENT DAY
# AT TRAIN TRIAL

Douglas Gordon GOODY
**30 YEARS**

Brian Arthur FIELD
**25 YEARS**

Roger CORDREY
**20 YEARS**

Leonard Dennis FIELD
**25 YEARS**

William BOAL
**24 YEARS**

John Denby WHEATER
**3 YEARS**

## PLAQUE IN MEMORY OF THE TRIAL

## THE BUCKS HERALD

ARE you interested in making the very best of your home?

Of course you are.

And the special 14-page Better Homes Supplement to be included with next week's HERALD is the very thing to keep you up-to-the-minute in all aspects of home making.

Finance, Building, Architecture, Furnishing, Heating, Decorating, Legal Points, Building Societies are just a few of the subjects discussed by specialists.

It all adds up to a KING SIZE HERALD next week. And, of course, the price remains UNCHANGED AT 3d. To make sure of a copy ORDER NOW.

## Died after being found unconscious

A MAN who was found unconscious in a boarding house room on Sunday morning died early the next day.

He was Mr. Roland Charles Clow (30), a shipwright, of The Canal Basin, Aylesbury.

On Saturday evening Mr. Clow took a room at The Willows, Buckingham Road, Aylesbury.

Attempts to rouse him for Sunday breakfast failed and a doctor was called.

Mr. Clow was taken to Stoke Mandeville Hospital where he died early on Monday without regaining consciousness.

himself that it was all over, he went on to say 'More worthy jurors I cannot imagine could have been found' and he exempted all twelve from jury service for life. Finally he said 'You and I have sat here together for so long that life without you will never seem quite the same'.

Life for the robbers was never quite the same either. Although three men who called themselves 'The Voice of the People' obtained 200 signatures to a petition asking for the sentences to be reduced to more humane proportions, they got nowhere. The law had to show that a crime of such magnitude as the Great Train Robbery had to be paid for.

In the Millwright Arms in Walton Street where the press used to gather, they unveiled a plaque to those who had 'wined and dined and died'. All top brass police and the press that had been involved signed it.

But the Great Train Robbery was not really over for a good many years to come. There were escapes and more sentencing and releases from jail. Ronald Biggs escaped after serving only a year of his thirty year sentence and lived a good life in South America, frequently providing the press with even more headlines. The escape of Charlie Wilson was said to have been organised by the man they called 'Mr Big'. The robbers said he was none other than Otto Skorzeny, the daring German paratrooper who had rescued Benito Mussolini, the Italian fascist dictator, from captivity in 1943, which was judged to be one of the most daring exploits of the Second World War. Wilson managed to stay free for some two years, but was then arrested in Montreal.

The town of Aylesbury seemed flat and quiet in the aftermath of the greatest trial in its history and little Cheddington went gently back to sleep.

# Burning for the Vote!

★

The Suffragist movement, intent on obtaining votes for women, really began in the last century, when a number of local committees were formed to organise demands for such a vote. In 1897 these were linked together to form the National Union of Women's Suffrage Societies and, in 1903, impatient Emmeline Pankhurst broke away from this organisation and formed the Women's Social and Political Union. She had long felt that the non-militant Suffragist movement lacked a certain vitality and needed a change of tactics. The members of this new Union were called Suffragettes and were filled with enthusiasm and excitement when their leader, Mrs Pankhurst, exhorted 'There is something that Governments care far more for than human life and that is the security of property, and so it is through property that we shall strike the enemy. Be militant each in your own way!'

Edwardian society was shocked to the core, especially when the Suffragettes deliberately drew public attention by heckling at meetings and chaining themselves to the railings of Buckingham Palace and Downing Street. They went on to organise a window smashing demonstration in Oxford Street. The most startling act of all was when one of their leaders, Emily Davison, died as she threw herself under the King's horse whilst it was galloping towards a victory in the Derby at Epsom.

These early Suffragettes suffered for their cause. They were often arrested and sent to prison where some went on 'hunger strike' and were forcibly fed.

Prior to the First World War in 1913, branches of the non-militant NUWSS were formed in Buckingham-shire, holding meetings and lectures. Believe it or not, there were also anti-suffrage meetings similar to the one held by the National League for Opposing Women's Suffrage at Marlow in January of that year. This meeting passed a resolution that there was not a clear enough demand from the electorate to warrant votes for women. At another meeting held at Beaconsfield by this opposing faction, a gentleman went one step further when he had the temerity to state (as quoted in the *Bucks Free Press*) 'Many women have not the mental or physical capability or the time to make good politicians – and, if they had the time, they are going to make very poor and shiftless home-keepers.' Courageous if not tactful!

The actions of Mrs Pankhurst's girls were by now well-known, and the first sign that militant suffragettes were in action in South Bucks came in the *Times* of 11th March 1913 with the headline 'RAILWAY INCENDIARISM – STATION BURNED DOWN' and in the *Bucks Free Press* of 14th March there appeared the astounding story of the gutting by fire of Saunderton Station on the Great Western line between High Wycombe and Princes Risborough.

The Station had been built around the turn of the century to service not only the village of Saunderton but also those of Bledlow Ridge, Lacey Green, Loosley Row and Speen. It soon became the main point of arrival and departure for travellers to those places. Saunderton did not possess a resident Police Officer, the nearest being a Constable stationed at Bledlow Ridge, and the railway authorities did not deem it necessary to leave staff on duty at the Station overnight due to the small amount of traffic passing through.

The night of 9th March was dark and stormy. The sort of night to lend itself to any deed of stealth and destruction. The Station Master left all secure and made his way home.

Just after 1 am, a cottager close by was awakened by what seemed to be hailstones pattering on her bedroom window. It turned out to be fragments from the burning railway station carried by a strong wind that was blowing.

Other cottagers were immediately roused and soon on the scene, including the Station Master, who had been dragged from his bed. From a telephone in the signal box, the Fire Brigades of Princes Risborough and High Wycombe were called. By the time they arrived the 'building was roaring like a furnace' and both structure and contents were beyond saving. The firemen worked feverishly, but when eventually the fire was beaten, nothing but the blackened walls remained.

All the undelivered parcels in the Parcel Office were completely destroyed as was the ticket office. Coins of gold, silver and copper contained in the safe were melted into one molten mass.

The *Bucks Free Press* found it curious to note that, despite the great heat, the clock, which hung on the wall in the centre of the Station, was still going and showed the correct time.

With the daylight came the discovery of two placards suspended from the railings at the Station entrance 'which pointed to the authorship of the outrage.' They read: 'VOTES FOR WOMEN' and 'BURNING TO GET THE VOTE'.

In the light of this, no less a figure than the Chief Constable of Bucks hurried to the scene together with other important members of his force. Someone remembered that two well-dressed women had been seen in the neighbourhood the previous day and had taken tea at a house not far from the Station before setting off in a motor car. The Fire Brigade then recalled that, whilst on their way to the fire, they had passed a strange young woman in the Bradenham Road. It was therefore concluded that the fire was without a doubt the work of militant suffragettes.

On that same Monday morning, approximately twelve miles away, part of Croxley Green Station was consumed by fire. Once again the flames spread rapidly and reduced the waiting rooms and offices to a heap of ruins. A short while prior to the outbreak, two women were seen half a mile from the Station walking towards Rickmansworth.

The Buckinghamshire countryside was agog at the news. The Saunderton Station fire had the effect of breaking up an open air meeting of the Wycombe Branch of the non-militant NUWSS due to the fact that the people were thoroughly confused by the two suffrage societies. As reported by the *Bucks Free Press*, at this meeting a Miss Coyle was the speaker and she started off well enough, but after a while orange peel and banana skins were thrown. Despite this, Miss Coyle carried on manfully (or womanfully) expounding upon 'Votes for women from an economic standpoint', until her audience began calling out about the fire at Saunderton and making insulting assertions that it was a pity she had not been thrown into it, followed by guffaws of merriment. It soon became impossible for her voice to be heard above the din.

After a certain amount of order had been restored, the lady tried desperately to reassure the crowd that the Society she represented had nothing to do with fires anywhere and were not militant to any degree. But the crowd rushed her and she was pushed to the ground.

Luckily she was rescued but forced to seek refuge in a nearby shop.

On the afternoon of 14th May 1913, a well-known portly lady from High Wycombe, the very essence of respectability, together with her equally respectable lady friend, journeyed to the village of Penn in order to call at a house near the Parish Church. On finding there was no-one at home, the two ladies decided to enter the Church and look around. 'Imagine their dismay' said the *Bucks Free Press* 'to discover that flames were coming from the direction of the organ'. Needless to say, they immediately raised the alarm among the villagers who managed to keep the flames in check with buckets of water whilst the ladies sped off to the vicarage to inform the Vicar, who picked up his cassock and ran to the Church where he feverishly rang the bells. The High Wycombe Fire Brigade had little trouble extinguishing the fire and, after all was safe, the Vicar turned to the Bible on the lectern for support only to suffer yet another shock. Placed inside the good book was a newspaper cutting headed 'Suffragette Incendiarism' and 'The Suffragette Cause'.

The two ladies, after such an afternoon fraught with excitement, headed for home by way of Tylers Green Common and by chance met Constable Young. They informed him that the Church was on fire and that he was wanted urgently by the Vicar. 'Judge our surprise' one lady is quoted as saying 'when the Constable coolly walked us back to the Church and detained us.'

There is absolutely no doubt that both ladies were suspected of starting the fire, based on police reasoning that as the fire had not had time to obtain much of a hold, the guilty persons could not be far away. An Inspector and Superintendent arrived from Beaconsfield. A gentleman who happened to be cycling through

Penn at the time, recognised the lady at once, and endeavoured to convince the Police that she was the last person to have committed such an outrage, but the ladies were not released. Unbelieved and frustrated, he telephoned the lady's husband and her doctor. The doctor turned up in his motor car and emphatically added his references. Still the two suspects were not released. Local landowner Sir Philip Rose went so far as to offer to stand bail.

Tea was provided in the vestry and both ladies made as comfortable as possible. However, they were not allowed to go until 11.30 that night.

The *Bucks Free Press* later stated:

'We are in a position to state that the Wycombe lady who had such an unpleasant experience has no sympathy with the militant suffragettes, nor has her lady friend. They will long remember the experience when a pleasant country walk ended in over five hours detention by the minions of the law.'

Then, in June, the non-militant NUWSS, in order to convince the Government that there was strong demand for votes for women from all over the country, organised 'The Great Women's Suffrage Pilgrimage'. The *Bucks Free Press* reported that 'from every point in our country women have come forward to join it.'

The pilgrimage started at Carlisle and, at the same time, another began at Lands End – their aim to reach Hyde Park on 26th July where they intended to hold various meetings and a special service in St Paul's. Those from the north were expected to arrive at Gerrards Cross Common on 24th July when friends and sympathisers would cheer them on their way.

Via Oxford and Thame, the first town the gallant pilgrims entered in the County of Buckinghamshire was Princes Risborough. Their coming had been previously

*The suffragettes at West Wycombe, before continuing their pilgrimage towards London. They were joined here by many supporters from Buckinghamshire. (Bucks Museum)*

announced and quite a crowd of people from the town and surrounding districts had assembled in the Market Square and a short meeting was held. All was orderly and the ladies, some on foot, some on bicycles, set off to march to West Wycombe. One mother of ten had cycled all the way from Bolton.

They arrived at West Wycombe around teatime, looking tired and rather dishevelled. 'Bannerettes' had now joined them from Chesham, Aylesbury, Wendover, Hampden and Stoke Mandeville, together with a number of recruits.

113

They gathered to listen to the strident voices of their leaders who demanded the vote and gave lengthy and varied reasons for doing so. Afterwards a much needed substantial tea was served at 'The Black Boy' and at half past six there was yet another forceful address followed by a general muster and roll call. Then, bearing banners aloft with such slogans as 'NO TAXATION WITHOUT REPRESENTATION', 'WE HAVE NOTHING TO FEAR FROM FREEDOM' and 'JUSTICE IS EVER THE BEST POLICY' they set off for the town of High Wycombe to the strains of a marching song. However, it must be stated that before they left 'there were indications that the marchers would encounter trouble before they reached the town, as a report from a trustworthy source was circulated to the effect that in the metropolis there had been an exceptional demand for tomatoes and stale eggs. After events proved the truth of this assertion.'

Along the road many youths were determined to have their bit of fun, but Sergeant Haynes scattered them in all directions. Despite this, as the ladies progressed along the way, the crowds were soon so dense as to make it almost impossible for them to make any kind of headway. Here and there they were greeted by waving handkerchiefs and cheers, but all too often this was drowned by jeers and hoots.

In Oxford Street it was estimated the crowds were 10,000 strong and the space on the fountain where it was intended a meeting should take place was packed 'almost to suffocation.' It was at this point that 'the rowdies let themselves go' shouting and throwing various missiles. Although hastily joined by reserves there seemed little the Police could do.

Courageous speakers mounted the platform (a lorry) headed by Miss Dove, Headmistress of the Abbey

School. But it was clearly obvious from the outset that there was not going to be any meeting. Councillor after Councillor appealed for order and implored the crowd to 'act like Englishmen'. Their answer was a volley of tomatoes and rotten eggs, some of which found their mark with precision. Sawdust saturated in oil and bags of flour flew through the air and banners were ripped to pieces. The Police were pushed from pillar to post and an indignant Constable Smith was tripped and slightly injured. There was a good half hour of this appalling behaviour with many a bold rush by the crowd to overturn the lorry platform.

It was with great risk that the speakers got away; the task of freeing themselves from the crowd was difficult and hazardous. Miss Dove managed to escape by way of Temple End but was forced to seek shelter at a residence along the way. The Suffragettes bore their afflictions marvellously and carried themselves with 'undaunted pluck.'

The rioters then made a rush on the offices of Messrs Baines, but the Police were soon masters of that situation.

From the steps of his house a local doctor addressed the crowd who then gave a hearing to two of the ladies who explained that their organisation was completely opposed to violence. The mob then 'got wind' of where the ladies' motors and luggage were housed and, under cover of darkness, a number of stones were thrown and windows broken. It was not until eleven o'clock that the police managed to clear the streets. 'Thus ended' said the *Bucks Free Press* 'one of the most disgraceful scenes ever witnessed in Wycombe.'

After attending a service in the Parish Church the next morning, the pilgrims resumed their journey to Penn with the indomitable Miss Dove well up front. As they passed through Terriers, one old local man called out 'Go home and wash your dirty clothes' but on marched the battle-scarred heroines. A meeting was held on the Common at Penn which was comparatively peaceful and although a few rotten eggs were thrown, none reached their target. Sergeant West calmly and with authority strolled slowly around until an egg of 'ancient date' passed over his head. He then forcefully interviewed three young men who innocently denied all knowledge. On the whole, the speakers were unhindered and it was not long before the whole contingent moved off to complete their journey.

However, it seemed that 'suffragette incendiarism' was not over. In the early hours of the morning of 15th August, in the pretty hillside village of Sands close by High Wycombe, an unoccupied house suddenly burst into flames. It was quickly brought under control but later, discovered in a cupboard under the stairs, were four rubber hot water bottles containing paraffin together with wax candles, matches and various other items which had been used to start the fire. A copy of *The Suffragette* was found in the grounds outside the house and entry had been gained through a scullery window.

A certain High Wycombe grocer lost no time in inserting the following opportune advertisement:

'Advice to Government re Suffragettes
Don't Forcibly feed them – give them Picton's
bacon and eggs. They'll offer no resistance.'

It was the 1914-18 war that gave impetus to the Suffragist cause. During that time women threw themselves wholeheartedly into a wide variety of jobs that they had never tackled before. They worked as bus conductors, on the land and in munitions, even serving in the armed forces. They proved their capabilities beyond all doubt and at the same time ran their homes alone and reared their children. By 1918 they had won over most of their opponents and a grateful Government could do no more than give women the vote, but then only to women over thirty who were house-holders, or the wives of householders.

Ten years later in 1928, complete victory was won and the Equal Franchise Act gave the vote to all women over the age of twenty-one for parliamentary and municipal elections.

117

# The Aylesbury
# Booze-up

★

The manner in which the Aylesbury Borough elections of the early 19th century were conducted was always considered quite scandalous. What with bribery, 'treating' and widespread drunkenness, it was not surprising that the town became well-known over the rest of the country for the wanton corruption that existed at such times. The people and electors of the town looked forward to an election with pleasurable anticipation; not only would they have a great time, but most of them would be considerably better off financially, particularly the 'potwallers'. This ancient privilege of the right to a parliamentary vote was afforded to any householder who could claim to boil his own pot; namely, any man who had a separate hearth on which could be cooked the food for his family. These 'potwallers' knew just how important they were to an aspiring member of parliament and expected to be bribed and 'treated' accordingly.

Democracy under such conditions was not served in any way, for a candidate needed to be very wealthy indeed to pay for all the bribes, dinners and drink needed to ensure that he was successful, which completely rules out a man perhaps possessed of much more competence but less money. As the *Bucks Herald* commented:

'A candidate is regarded as a rich booty and prize to

be made the most of. His pockets are pulled at by his 'friends' from all sides. He sees burdensome debts contracting daily against him. But he must not breathe a complaint – he is in the hands of his Committee. They for the time are the lords of his substance. At their nod, daily feasts are spread for a whole month at a public house, and streams of gratuitous brandy and water set constantly flowing.'

Not many could pay for 25 breakfasts and 384 dinners for freeholders plus beer, wine, port, sherry, rum and brandy as listed in a bill from 'The White Hart' received by a candidate in 1818. And that was just for the first day of the poll! In those days the poll for boroughs could remain open for a week and that for the county up to 14 days, thus ensuring that voters from the outlying parts had time to reach the polling station. The streets sometimes became completely impassable as farm wagons, carriages, gigs, stage coaches, post-chaises, tradesmen's carts, etc. all jostled and bustled for position. The longer the poll remained open, the more money changed hands and, more often than not, a successful candidate would find himself the subject of a petition to the Aylesbury Election Committee launched by an opposing party stating that his election was invalid due to corruption. If the charges were really bad and proved against him, he would find himself unseated, and yet another election and poll would take place, which did not displease the people and 'potwallers' one bit.

In fact, things were so bad at the beginning of the 19th century that a weary Aylesbury Election Committee called for the serious attention of the House of Commons to the notorious and longstanding system of corruption known to exist there. The House did not need to be told. They had long been fed up with it.

Scarcely an election had been held in the town without one party petitioning another, and some newly elected member hardly had time to make his maiden speech before being unseated – and had not that town returned one of the most troublesome members ever to enter the House – John Wilkes?

Some members of the House felt strongly disposed to disfranchise the Borough completely, but local influence prevailed and in 1804 the House, thinking that a new influx of a different class of voter would improve matters, came up with a Bill that allowed the people of the surrounding Hundreds of Aylesbury to vote in an Aylesbury Borough Election. This meant that every man owning a freehold in the Borough or Hundreds of Aylesbury had the right to vote. It appears to have made little difference, although it did suppress the 'potwalloping' interest to some extent.

Petitions of protest still flew backwards and forwards after an Election and one man giving evidence before the Election Committee told how candidates and their agents had set up at the various inns. He stated that he was ushered into a room where stood two bowls on a large table, one containing punch – the other guineas. Names were checked from a list and, if a man had been free of parish relief for a year, he was entitled to vote. Three guineas were given to him and a glass of punch. He then drank the 'gentleman's' health whilst at the same time professing wide-eyed ignorance as to who the 'gentleman' was who was so very generous.

He was asked 'Didn't the punch make you drunk?' 'Drunk?! Lord bless you, no Sir! How could it? I was drunk 'afore I went!'

By 1832, Parliamentary reform was well under way and boroughs like Amersham and Wendover were disfranchised; but not Aylesbury. Under the new

*An average election night party around the end of the 18th century.*
(Mansell Collection)

Reform Act, those 'potwallers' then in existence were still permitted the right to vote, but no new ones admitted. Gradually over the years the 'potwallers' dwindled away until not one was living. But even after this, the chicanery and fun still went on.

Nomination Day was full of excitement and, such was the confusion and uproar when a candidate rose to make a speech that it often appeared he was miming! Hecklers were really hecklers in those days and made their opinions well felt. They seemed to be in possession of the most deep buried details of a man's private life and did not hesitate to call them out. Colours or 'favours' were given away and bands played as loud as they could.

After the declaration of the Poll, a flushed successful candidate was chaired through the town. He balanced on a stout chair covered in his colours or that of his party, and the bearers were required to be pretty hefty fellows ready to protect their man against attacks by the defeated party as they processed through the town behind the band. It was usually at this time that the band played 'See the conquering hero comes' which proved too much to bear for the other side and hostilities would invariably break out. J.K. Fowler recounts in his *Records of Old Times* how he saw some desperate fights with more than a hundred taking part when the new MP was forcibly ejected from the chair and pitched headlong into the crowd.

But it was the Borough election of 1850 that is known to this day as 'The Big Booze-Up'. It all began in December of that year and every turn of event was ably reported by both the *Bucks Herald* and the *Bucks Advertiser*. There had been many meetings in the chain of events leading up to Nomination and Polling Days. The Nomination meeting was held in the County Hall on 26th December. The moment the doors were opened hordes of people of all shapes and sizes rushed in, until the spacious room was filled to capacity; 'every nook and cranny being occupied by human beings, all eager to witness and join in the general confusion of the day.'

The noise was so great that it was some time before the Reverend Harrison could find the courage to rise to his feet, let alone make himself heard. He proposed Mr Frederick Calvert as a fit and proper person to represent the Borough and Hundreds of Aylesbury. This brought forth absolute pandemonium and cries of 'Send him to the New Drop' (the new hanging place in the town) which could not have filled the waiting candidate with confidence. This was followed by 'Go Home', and 'Go back, Calvert, to your Masters'. The Proposer struggled to assure his audience of the soundness of the character

of his candidate (boos and hisses) and his consistent
Protestant principles and how he was opposed to the
Pope in Rome. ('We don't want to hear about the Pope'
and 'Go Home'.) The remainder of the speech from the
Proposer was lost amid the din and he left the stage to
hisses and just a few cheers.

Mr John Houghton was then proposed as a candidate
amid cheers and hisses. Mr Gibbs seconded and
pleaded Mr Houghton's case with eloquence. He
courageously informed the meeting that 'We have gone
back twenty years in the conduct of this election and in
the introduction of bribery, treating, music and ribands'
(utter confusion). Mr Gibbs was not to be outdone.
'Those who have the guinea tickets make the most
noise'. (Hisses and cheers.) Mr Gibbs, becoming bolder
by the minute, stated that 'some of Mr Calvert's agents
were the most drunken, swindling gamblers the world
ever produced'. (Unbelievable uproar and 'Name them,
Name them, etc.'.) This unbridled tumult went
unchecked for some time until a Mr Hamilton stood up
and said that as he considered the whole affair an
absolute farce, he nominated Mr Punch. (Laughter.)

Candidate Mr Frederick Calvert swallowed hard and
stood up to address the crowds. He was a tenant farmer
and a Whig so it was natural that he should begin by
recounting all the good things brought about by that
party and asked the audience to look at the reforms
they had made. He said he did not come to make
promises ('Go home then') and he referred to the
aggressive attitude of the Pope. ('Never mind the
Pope.') His motto was 'Hard work – good pay – No
work – no pay' (hisses and boos). He was for free trade
in everything. ('Snuff and Bacca'.) In his opinion the
existing game laws were infamous and he felt that any
man should be allowed to kill game on his own

property. He touched on all the popular items, but try as he might he could not capture or please his audience.

Mr Houghton then stood forward, and he was received with loud applause and just a few expressions of opposition. He did not have very kind things to say of Mr Calvert, who in his opinion was only where he was due to high influence within the county. He ventured to say that Calvert was surrounded by fawning sycophants who would do anything for filthy lucre. (Cheers.) Mr Houghton assured his audience that he too was for Free Trade (once again, 'Snuff and Bacca'). He hinted at the bribery performed in the election and said that he left it to the honest voters to decide who was the better man (a voice from the back of the hall – 'You're both good looking').

Mr Calvert indignantly rose to reply to some of Mr Houghton's remarks, but he was received with a volley of boos and hisses.

As the *Bucks Herald* reported 'The uproar now assumed a somewhat furious character, the table at which the representatives of the press were seated was besieged and everything was in disorder and confusion'.

Polling commenced the next morning at 8 o'clock and closed at 4 o'clock in the afternoon. The surprising result was:

Calvert . . . 488, Houghton . . . 190

So it did look as if some kind of persuasion had been afoot!

The *Bucks Herald* was both disgusted and indignant and on 4th January 1851 commented in an editorial 'a noisy mob, half drunk at the expense of Mr Calvert's party, prevented anything like order or business in the proceedings. Outrageous treating and ingenious bribery were the order of the day . . . the expense must have been enormous, even for Aylesbury, but it is understood it will not fall entirely on individuals'. They assured their readers 'there is little fear that these effects will secure more than a temporary triumph. The Borough and Hundreds of Aylesbury are not a marketable commodity'.

The following week under the caption 'CURIOUS COINCIDENCE' the paper remarked that it was not often that the statement of their rival, the *Bucks Advertiser*, ran parallel with their own, nor did they have any occasion to quote them, but the following paragraph so exactly confirmed their own testimony as to the proceedings of the last election that they were tempted to transcribe it. And they did:

'We are now removed just one week from the contest for the Borough representation. All the excitement is over. Mr Calvert is an MP, for which the Government is truly thankful. Many hundreds of pounds have been paid for the said honour . . . Public houses were opened as usual. Dinners, suppers, toddy, and tea as plentiful as ever. People were drunk on Monday, Tuesday, Wednesday, Thursday, Friday, Saturday and Sunday morning, gloriously drunk. We saw them in public houses drunk, rolling through the streets drunk, carried home by their wives drunk. And they were drunk not at their own expense. Publicans boast it was the best election they ever saw, for, say they, the money was paid down beforehand. We must also add that people wearing the cloth of gentlemen were drunk – not drunk as pigs are drunk, for pigs have more sense; but as far gone as ever men were who degrade themselves to a position lower than the lowest brute.'

On 17th March 1851 Calvert made his maiden speech in the House. On the 23rd an objection was lodged with the Aylesbury Election Committee as to the conduct of the last election. On 4th April the Chairman of that Committee announced their decision that Mr Calvert was not fairly or duly elected and he was unseated. Preparations were immediately begun for the next election and further boozing.

With various other Acts over the years, things improved democratically at Aylesbury and elections were conducted in a slightly more sober and upright manner. But nostalgia was felt for the fun and enjoyment of those riotous old elections for many years afterwards.

'These were the good old 'lection days,
The good old days of yore,
When every vote brought a ten pound note
And a barrel of beer to your door;
When golden guineas rained hard and fast,
And Boro's were bought with beer;
When the bowl went round till we rolled on
   the ground,
'Cause our heads were giddy and queer.'

                     – Old Aylesbury Song

# Index